Fixed Star in Mind: Set Goals, Achieve Goals

Philipp Plugmann

Fixed Star in Mind: Set Goals, Achieve Goals

Transformation of the Mindset

Philipp Plugmann
School of Health, Education and
Social Sciences
SRH University of Applied
Sciences
Heidelberg, Germany

ISBN 978-3-662-70718-0   ISBN 978-3-662-70719-7 (eBook)
https://doi.org/10.1007/978-3-662-70719-7

Translation from the German language edition: "Fixstern im Kopf: Ziele setzen, Ziele erreichen" by Philipp Plugmann, © Der/die Herausgeber bzw. der/die Autor(en), exklusiv lizenziert an Springer-Verlag GmbH, DE, ein Teil von Springer Nature 2021. Published by Springer Berlin Heidelberg. All Rights Reserved.

This book is a translation of the original German edition "Fixstern im Kopf: Ziele setzen, Ziele erreichen" by Philipp Plugmann, published by Springer-Verlag GmbH, DE in 2021. The translation was done with the help of an artificial intelligence machine translation tool. A subsequent human revision was done primarily in terms of content, so that the book will read stylistically differently from a conventional translation. Springer Nature works continuously to further the development of tools for the production of books and on the related technologies to support the authors.

© The Editor(s) (if applicable) and The Author(s), under exclusive license to Springer-Verlag GmbH, DE, part of Springer Nature 2025

This work is subject to copyright. All rights are solely and exclusively licensed by the Publisher, whether the whole or part of the material is concerned, specifically the rights of translation, reprinting, reuse of illustrations, recitation, broadcasting, reproduction on microfilms or in any other physical way, and transmission or information storage and retrieval, electronic adaptation, computer software, or by similar or dissimilar methodology now known or hereafter developed.
The use of general descriptive names, registered names, trademarks, service marks, etc. in this publication does not imply, even in the absence of a specific statement, that such names are exempt from the relevant protective laws and regulations and therefore free for general use.
The publisher, the authors and the editors are safe to assume that the advice and information in this book are believed to be true and accurate at the date of publication. Neither the publisher nor the authors or the editors give a warranty, expressed or implied, with respect to the material contained herein or for any errors or omissions that may have been made. The publisher remains neutral with regard to jurisdictional claims in published maps and institutional affiliations.

This Springer imprint is published by the registered company Springer-Verlag GmbH, DE, part of Springer Nature.
The registered company address is: Heidelberger Platz 3, 14197 Berlin, Germany

If disposing of this product, please recycle the paper.

Foreword

"Anyone who has visions should go to the doctor," is probably the most famous quote from the former Federal Chancellor Helmut Schmidt. One may rightly have differing opinions about the meaning of its content, however, the author of this work, Prof. Dr. Dr. Plugmann, has managed like few others to ultimately turn visions into actions—and he has also become a doctor in the process. I have known Prof. Plugmann for over ten years and we have also become very good friends. However, I am always amazed anew at how many professional challenges he consistently pursues and masters over long periods of time: work in his own dental practice, professorship, business consulting, third doctorate, publication of books… These are all essentially full-time jobs! What's great about him is that he doesn't live in a basement for this, but also leads a successful family life.

Do you finally want to unleash your full potential and not be distracted by unnecessary disturbances and concerns? Then the book in front of you is just right for you. Prof. Plugmann shares in it how he pursues his visions, translates these into concrete goals, implements them, and how you can adopt and adapt his thought patterns for your challenges.

Let yourself be inspired by Prof. Plugmann's thought patterns! I wish you much success in reading this work and implementing the recommendations for action contained therein.

www.glauner.info

Regensburg, Germany Patrick Glauner
Juni 2021

Preface Prof. Dr. Dr. Plugmann

Attention! This book is extremely dangerous and contagious!! It might ignite you and your power completely. One of the main side effects of this book is that you might unfold your full potential. In the worst case, you take full leadership and responsibility for setting and achieving your goals and from now on, you go full throttle for a very long time. This can turn into a chronic condition. You should be prepared to deal with recurring success experiences.

Friends, family, teachers, coaches, classmates, and lecturers—what I have had to listen to over the past decades. There were always people who meant well for me. My potential was limited, I wouldn't be able to do it, and the advice to please be realistic were some exemplary well-intentioned recommendations for my life. That bounced off me and giving up was never an issue—why should it be, the future was not yet written. And so I do my thing, I am a permanent learning and working machine and will step it up every year.

Dear readers, please do not let anyone convince you that you cannot learn, establish, or achieve anything. You can. The pre-analysis, organization, and implementation are crucial. In this, time is one of your trump cards. The success of reaching our guiding star lies within all of us, we have just been made to adopt the mental model that we fit into a certain box—this is a constructed illusion. The brain can learn anything and the human will can implement and create everything, you just need to calmly look around the world. I will try to support you with experiences, anecdotes, and a bit of science so that you can permanently unleash your full potential. Let's go!

I would like to thank Prof. Dr. Patrick Glauner, one of the youngest professors in Europe for Artificial Intelligence, for his foreword, and Prof. Dr. Sabrina Krauss and Ms. Assina Müller for their guest contributions. I am particularly grateful to Ms. Marion Krämer, Ms. Janina Tschech, and Ms. Margot Schlomski from Springer Gabler Verlag for their constructive support.

North Rhine-Westphalia　　　　　　　　　　　Philipp Plugmann
Germany

Contents

1 The Starting Shot to the Fixed Star — 1
  1.1 Success Means Growing Like a Tree — 15
  1.2 The Best 10% — 21
  1.3 The New Coach — 25
  1.4 The Written Form — 28
  1.5 Mental Flexibility — 30
  References — 34

2 Transformation of the Mindset — 37
  2.1 Attitude and Setting Goals — 38
  2.2 Setting High Goals — 41
  2.3 Self-motivation and Resilience — 46
  2.4 Good Conditions and Personal Dream — 50
  2.5 Long-Term Race — 56
  References — 60

3 Time — 61
  3.1 Time Protection—the Golden Weekend — 62
  3.2 Activate the Time Saw — 68

3.3	Innovation through the Individual Time Flow Diagram	70
3.4	Hyperactivity	78
3.5	Designing the Network	89
References		96

4 Accept Competition and go Full Throttle — 99

4.1	Sports Experiences and Professional Competition	100
4.2	Guest Commentary Assina Müller "(Team) Sports in Youth Toughens Up" (Former Handball Bundesliga Player, Master's Student and Physiotherapist, B. Sc.)	104
4.3	Principle of Highest Urgency	107
4.4	Expertise Wins: Knowledge of Products and Services	110
4.5	Guest Contribution RESILIENCE by Prof. Dr. Sabrina Krauss, SRH University in North Rhine-Westphalia	113
4.5.1	Resilience	113
References		117

5 The Decision for the Personal Innovation Process — 121

5.1	The 95/5 Rule	122
5.2	Discipline and Continuity	123
5.3	The Next Goal: Nothing is Older than Yesterday's Success!	135
5.4	Now Everything Depends on you—Give it Your All!	137
References		139

About the Author

Philipp Plugmann has been a Professor of Interdisciplinary Periodontology and Prevention in the Bachelor's program for Dental Hygienists at the SRH University of Health's Leverkusen campus since February 1, 2020. After studying dentistry at the University of Cologne and passing the state examination in 2000, he earned his doctorate in 2005, while establishing his practice, at the University Hospital Cologne in the Department of Oral, Maxillofacial and Facial Surgery. In addition, he completed a multi-year doctoral program in Medical Sciences at the Private University of the Principality of Liechtenstein (UFL) in 2013, while continuing his professional work.

He holds a Master of Science in Periodontology and Implant Therapy from the German Society for Periodontology (DGParo), a Master of Business Administration with a focus on Health Care Management, and a Master of Science in Business Innovation (both from EBS University for Business and Law). In total, he has published 80 publications in the fields of dentistry, innovation, and technology and has edited 7 books in both German and English. His books have been positively mentioned by CISCO, a major US technology company, the Federal Association of Small and Medium-Sized Enterprises (BVMW), and a long-standing professor in the field of innovation at the elite US university Berkeley. His second book in 2018, "Designing Innovation Environments," published by Springer Gabler Verlag, had over 100,000 chapter downloads in the first 30 months.

During his 22-year professional career as a dentist and implantologist, in addition to his dental practices in Leverkusen and Berlin, he founded 2 companies that deal with prevention and services in the healthcare sector, the development of surgical software for dental operations, and digital technologies. He has presented research results on innovations in healthcare at conferences including those at Harvard University (USA, East Coast), Berkeley University (USA, West Coast), the Max Planck Institute for Innovation and Competition (Munich), the Max Planck Institute for Social Law and Social Policy (Munich), and Nanyang Tech University (Singapore). In parallel to his practice, Prof. Dr. Dr. Philipp Plugmann was active for 12 years at universities in Karlsruhe, Cologne, and Bielefeld, where he also supervised and first-marked master's theses. From 2007 to 2016, he was a lecturer in the field of innovations at the Karlsruhe University of Applied Sciences—Technology and Business and was awarded by the rector for outstanding teaching.

Since 2013, he has been working as a Research Fellow at the University Dental Clinic Marburg in the Department of Periodontology and has been recognized there for his outstanding commitment due to his case reports, lectures, and international research presentations. He is currently working on his third doctoral thesis, is a reviewer for the Federal Health Gazette, and since 2019 has been a Senior Advisor in the field of Life Science and Health Care at an international technology consultancy.

1

The Starting Shot to the Fixed Star

The starting signal for your guiding star has been given, and I wish you to gain the maximum benefit from this entire book. Experience shows that when it comes to achieving personal life goals, it's best to rely on oneself and not on others. No one will come to rescue you, and the likelihood that someone will recognize your talent or potential on the way to your guiding star, take you by the hand and lead you to this star, is relatively low. Of course, it cannot be ruled out, but it's best to rely on yourself. This also saves you a lot of disappointments. Expecting nothing from others puts you in a relaxed state of mind. Once you have internalized the realization that you can only rely on yourself, or rather, you are the only person you can rely on 100%, you will realize that you are the only person who can take responsibility and leadership for achieving your goals, and no one else. This, in turn, leads to the realization that you must put yourself in a permanent state of mind where you are highly motivated and constantly working to exceed your own limits. This book aims to help you with this, whether your goals are small, medium or large, private, family, non-academic, academic or purely professional.

> **Tip**
> One of the most important points in all self-set goals is: **Never give up!**

Regardless of the current conditions and your self-assessed chances of achieving your goal, you must never give up. This also includes dealing with defeats, as defeats are full of learning opportunities. If you experience a defeat, whether it's a failed exam, a lost semester, a non-admission to a course of study, the rejection of a scientific submission, a failed relationship or a failed start-up, etc., each of these events has the potential to learn from it and do better next time. You can emotionally detach yourself from the defeats and view the extract positively, which you get when you simply look at this event soberly. This ultimately means that defeats can become part of the path to success. You have the opportunity to take a clear stand on what exactly you want in life, and you should be uncompromising towards yourself. Towards others, whether professionally or privately, one should always have an open, listening and compromise-oriented, cooperative nature, because you cannot deal with other people like a bull in a china shop, it works once, but people will probably turn away at some point because they simply want to avoid this situation. It is more effective to listen and try to negotiate a compromise. But you can be uncompromising towards yourself, honest and determined in the matter. And you can read how this works in the following. This does not mean that if someone treats you unfairly, professionally or privately, that you should simply endure it softly. You should also resist appropriately in private and professional environments and take a stand when the situation requires it. But the core of success lies within oneself. And that means, you should not make up excuses for yourself. To be able to do this well, everything depends on good planning, I call it the "rulebook".

The Rulebook
You can develop a rulebook for yourself by defining certain priorities. The first is setting the goal. After a certain period of consideration, you should take a stand and honestly formulate what exactly you want, whatever it may be. As in a car race or marathon, you should know the direction and finish line so that you can work towards this set goal and know when you have reached it. This can be an educational goal, a financial goal or a private matter, it can be the future founding of a small or large family, it can be happiness as a goal, it can be anything you want. This approach is independent of whether it is a small, medium or large goal.

It is important, if you are honest with yourself, that you define a large guiding star in the sky, on the horizon, and this is intended only for you. You also keep this for a long time just for yourself, this is also the magnet and energy supplier for the next years. Therefore, be completely honest with yourself and ask yourself:

- **What do I want?**

And then write it down, that is then point one on your very personal rulebook list. Point two on this list should be:

- **What am I willing to sacrifice and how obsessed am I with it?**

Here you have to ask yourself: What could I do without? And what must I do without in order to reach my goal? These can be certain habits, it can be a certain way of thinking, also about oneself, about life, the meaning of your future activities or the benefit for society. This can also lead to a reflection of self-assessment. It is important that you realize that only the renunciation of certain things at all constitutes the prerequisite to be able to reach this guiding star. The path to the goal, you also see at this point, leads through yourself and not through third parties. You are the guarantor of success, and everything revolves around your decisions. The path will be rocky, challenging and strenuous—you already know this now, and so you will not be surprised when the obstacles, in whatever form they may appear, cause you stress. If possible, stay emotionally cool and leave the field to your sober mind.

Basic Attitude

What was, was. You should let the past rest and make peace with it. There is no point in wasting energy or thoughts on the past, what could have been, who may have put obstacles in your way, or where you have failed on your own. That is history, water under the bridge, let it rest and leave it far behind you.

You can now focus all your energy on the future, and this third point, the individual basic attitude, is fundamental. You are allowed to develop an attitude where you realize that you can achieve your goals, regardless of how small or large these goals are. I would like to give you a little help with this.

1 The Starting Shot to the Fixed Star

When defining one's guiding star, whether it is to be achieved in three, ten, or twenty years, there is occasionally a certain fear in the background. The fear that one might not achieve the goal or fail. Thoughts like "What will others say" or "How will I look in the eyes of others if I don't achieve the goal?" can be safely ignored, because on the one hand, most other people are not interested in what you do, as they are busy with themselves, and on the other hand, if you risk nothing, you have already lost and deprived yourself of any chance. Do not let this emotion of fear guide you, but use your mind and do what you should do to achieve the goal. No one can take away the risk of failure from you.

I would like to tell you how I internalized a lesson on the subject of "fear of challenges and possible failure":

When I had double admission for human medicine and dentistry in Cologne after my high school graduation and medical test in 1990, I worked for the first three years as a student nurse in the high-rise building of the University Hospital Cologne to finance my studies. Although I later put my studies in human medicine on hold because I decided to learn certain interdisciplinary competencies and start a company parallel to my dental studies. But the day and night shifts, especially during the semester breaks, in the various departments, whether it was oral, maxillofacial and facial surgery, the emergency room or otolaryngology, brought me into contact with cancer patients, specifically with cancer patients who were undergoing palliative medical therapy or were about to undergo it. In other words, the cancer was inoperable and it was a question of time whether the patients would live another six months or two years, but these were people who were mentally close to death and knew that they would die in the foreseeable future.

Especially during my night shifts, when it was a bit quieter at the university hospital for an hour or two, which is rather rare at university hospitals, one could empathize very deeply with the people's thoughts in a one-on-one conversation and one of the insights of these people, as I personally experienced it, was simply that they did not trust themselves enough and did not do certain things out of shame or fear of how it would look in the eyes of family, friends or further acquaintances. These were very different things. Some wanted to study art, another wanted to become a carpenter, the fourth wanted to become a truck driver, another wanted to start a large family, wanted to have ten children. Another wanted to travel the world for five years. I can't list all the things that were mentioned to me, but when you are close to death or have a near-death experience, the way of thinking seems to be different.

It is possible to learn from the experiences of other people. I did that back then. In the conversations, one seems to develop a very clear mind regarding the priorities and really important things in life very quickly when close to death. I experienced the same thing regularly in the conversations with relatives, in which I was accompanying the chief physicians. The relatives also had a "mindshift" (Engl. mind shift). I personally experienced it as if the affected persons or their relatives had awakened from a state of trance and could suddenly see everything differently and clearly.

These experiences moved me at the time to also visit other courses of study on the campus of the University of Cologne, their lectures, libraries or events. My interest in the various disciplines was always very broad, I was interested in many things out of pure curiosity, not only in dentistry, which I love to do, but after three years I decided to put my studies in human medicine on hold to also deal with other subject areas. Life can be so short that you can simply follow your heart and gut feeling without a guilty conscience. Inner joy in what one learns and does, fun and peace of mind are hard to press into an economic balance, but certainly for an emotional balance.

What I simply want to pass on to you as an experience is, you don't have to wait until you are close to death, although I would like to note here that there is no guarantee for anything, you can be run over by a truck tomorrow or fall ill with a serious illness and then that's it, but you have to realize that you are the captain of your own life, or the captain of your own life, and that you have all the chances ahead of you and should not be afraid to set a small or large goal, because there is also a lot of joy in life and fun in getting a little closer to this goal year by year. If you approach things with fun, good humor and confidence, then you don't constantly look at the clock and stay away from mental exhaustion.

Self-Appreciation

Over the past decades, now being 50 years young and having had the opportunity to meet many people, I have found that it is not a given to have a high level of self-appreciation. I can only affirm you positively, you are unique, you are fantastic and special. You are on this planet and everything is possible. If one can believe the average life expectancy figures, even for those who are just being born, still very few will live to be over 100 years old, so you have several decades ahead of you where you can be productive, and that is actually a manageable time, a limited time, and it is your good right, firstly to develop a high appreciation for yourself and secondly to set your goals accordingly, independently of the views and opinions of others.

Even if you are currently in a position or job where you say "but I am only in this and that position". This has nothing to do with the design and success prognosis of your future. Your future is not yet written, you can shape everything positively and you should cultivate a high self-appreciation.

Poulsen (2006) and Hitzenberger and Schuett (2016) describe in their publications the importance of self-appreciation, self-care and burnout prevention. It becomes clear that professional self-confidence has a strong influence on one's own positive emotional world and that the individual should not overstrain their own limits in the context of self-care in order to prevent exhaustion and burnout.

As so often in life, no rule without exception, sometimes one can briefly, for a few days or weeks, dip into the exhaustion area to reach the goal and can lie down on the ground behind the finish line like a performance athlete and regenerate. From my personal experience, this is ultimately a matter of training, one can get to know and expand one's limits over the years.

Performance

The best basis for assessment for oneself and one's environment is performance. There is no way around it. We live in a performance society and in a performance society, performance counts. Physically, of course, performance is defined as work over time, which means you should go full throttle, work a lot, invest many hours, days, weeks, months, years to achieve a corresponding level of performance, and in addition, the question of work intensity, how intensively you use the time, also plays a role.

The idea that you can just sit out the time will not work. You should seize the opportunity to be very active towards the pole star, develop outstanding commitment, work a lot, hard and intensively, then you will achieve your goals. In our performance society, just like in football, only results count—that's the reality. The fact that this is unfair, resource-draining and without any guarantee of success is also part of reality. Thus, a reason to give more full throttle and not to slacken.

Gündel et al. (2014) show that working, pursuing one's goals and staying healthy do not have to be opposites. Kraaz (2021) shows how to remain sustainably efficient in order to master the business marathon. Both authors also emphasize that good planning is a key aspect of success in addition to core performance.

Proper Communication with Partners
The path to your guiding star, the path to your success, only leads through tough decisions. And the fact that you should make decisions is inevitable. If you do not make decisions or postpone them for too long, it will cost you time and, in the worst case, rob you of all motivation. One of the decisions you need to make is:

- **Have I communicated well with the partner at my side?**

There is nothing worse than an asymmetrical motivation gradient in the attitude within a partnership. This means that one person is going full throttle, seven days a week, pursuing the guiding star hard through high learning and work effort, through commitment even on weekends and in the evenings, and the other person feels neglected or not taken along on the path due to insufficient or inadequate communication from this partner. One should avoid demotivating one's partner to the point where cracks appear in the relationship due to one's own performance behavior.

You could regularly arrange joint outings, walks, or time intervals where you talk about the goals, what has been achieved so far, and the resulting benefits for the family. This could lead to the partnership enduring and both of you positively heading towards this guiding star. You can ask yourself:

What do I need to do to reach my guiding star and strengthen the partnership?

Have you done your homework to design the time, planning, and implementation overview in such a way that your partnership grows and strengthens at the same time?

This is a very strenuous task, but ultimately you should not risk your partnership for your goal, your guiding star, on the contrary, you take people, partners, friends, and family, into the boat through preventive and continuous communication, even into your inner circle, who support you, but at least understand why you are pursuing this goal, and virtually let you breathe, to contribute towards this goal.

> **Tip**
>
> Yes, do it. Maintain continuous communication before, during, and after reaching the guiding star. This strengthens love, friendships, and family. Everyone understands and feels like your companions, what could be nicer than going a long way together and successfully—and having fun doing it!

My lawyer friends would say at this point: "Yes, Philipp, although you have no legal claim to fun in life or fun at work, but yes, you have the right to shape everything in your favor."

And, let's be honest, you are doing other people a favor by communicating well, instead of ending up in constant conflicts about why you are doing this on Saturday or that on Sunday, or why you are reading or writing something for two hours before going to bed. This is your task and you should take this responsibility.

Therefore, I always recommend seeking conversation and simply explaining to the other people you live with that you have a big goal that you prioritize, that you are trying to go the way on your own because you can only rely on yourself when achieving this goal. And that requires a high work effort over many months and years. And you should also explain that this ultimately benefits the partnership and possibly the family, because success ultimately opens up long-term opportunities that naturally also benefit the family.

This is not about financial matters, it's simply about having more time for the family later, if you have been going full throttle for ten, twenty years, you can certainly, once you have reaped the fruits, then also have more time resources for the family and enable certain things.

With good communication with your environment, you will feel that there is progress and a willingness to compromise. I think it's just fair to inspire people until they are just as positively minded, to live in a society where you can communicate your dreams and work on them, to achieve this through a strong commitment over many years, and they will support you. This can even become a turbo booster if you are in a relationship where you strengthen, support, and motivate each other, then suddenly one plus one becomes three. This is also an aspect you should think about.

In the scientific literature on the practical problem often discussed as "career or family", there are exciting aspects that I would like to illustrate for you. Hancke et al. (2011)

showed in a survey of a total of 4564 gynecologists, of which 2830 (62%) were female, that especially female gynecologists wish for extra-familial childcare in order to have better conditions for desired leadership positions.

Rusconi and Solga (2011) examined the intertwining of professional careers and family in academic partnerships, addressing the fact that both partners strive for a career and describe the challenges where constructive communication with each other can have a positive influence. Ihsen et al. (2008) describe in the VDI report how engineers can cope with the tension between profession, career, and family. The study, consisting of a qualitative and quantitative part, conducted a survey among graduates of engineering courses, executives, and companies. Some results were that large companies have professionalized offers to enable staff to reconcile work and family, and that employees tend to take shorter parental leave to meet the expectations of employers. But also problematic things like the assignment of family-friendliness, old-fashioned role distributions, and conditions for achieving leadership positions were highlighted.

Althaber et al. (2011) describe the issue of "career with child in science" the problem of childcare, personal aspiration, and those of successful women and their partners, Rödl (2010) presents the compatibility of career and family as part of the law firm Rödl & Partner, and the organizational establishment of company kindergartens and nurseries.

The exemplary scientific literature shows the challenges, and my practical recommendation is: talk to your partner. Draw a common path where the private and professional desires of both parties can be reconciled. Together you are strong!

Social Commitment

When you have reached your guiding star one day (nothing is older than yesterday's success, so you have to create the next guiding star), then you also have a moral obligation to give something back to society, in whatever form. Some call this social commitment, others charity. Regardless of how you label it, if you were fortunate enough to grow up in a society like ours, where everything was made possible for you by the constitution and the rule of law, through educational and development opportunities, through your family and friends, kindergarten teachers, teachers, professors, trainers, and countless supporters, whoever, paved the way for you, even if you were the main driving force at the core, it is good to engage socially for society. My wife and I started about ten years ago to financially support certain organizations, institutions, universities, and projects. These were not gigantic amounts, sometimes 1000 euros, sometimes 2000 euros, sometimes more, depending on the project, but we have an agreement in the family that we owe our success to society and it gives us great pleasure to give something back. Social commitment can also be voluntary activities. For example, I am also active as a volunteer mentor for start-ups or have organized certain activities. There are many diverse opportunities, it's not always just a money donation, it can also be a material donation or time, if you engage voluntarily; and volunteering in Germany is very broad, you can excellently contribute to society and others. Because ultimately the last shirt has no pockets, so you can't take any of your financial wealth with you and also leave a role model function and possibly motivate others to also get involved voluntarily or financially and support the society that has enabled you to develop as you have developed.

The scientific literature has numerous studies and contributions to show on the motives of social engagement. Schulze (2009) examined the motives, goals, and values of founders. He works out differences between gender-specific and personality-specific orientations. Heinze and Strünck (2001) describe the relevance of voluntary social engagement and show potentials and promotion possibilities.

Regardless of your personal motives, your action by engaging socially also has a positive influence on your environment and the community in which you live. This strengthens the community and you can live up to your role model function, if you wish to do so.

Integrity, Loyalty, and Reliability

On the way to success, you depend on interaction with people, and for these people to have the security that you are reliable, loyal, and integral, you have to live it. This means, things that are discussed with you, you keep confidentially for yourself, if you have given your word that a certain thing will be done, then you do it, and if for some reason it doesn't work out, then you explain why and why, and also bring a solution approach with you.

People should have the certainty with you that you do not gossip about things that have been entrusted to you and that they can rely on you. This element, that you are also a character trait or image building block someone who is considered reliable, or someone who implements projects or who sticks to goals over a long period of time and achieves them, will help you on the way to win people over for projects, to inspire these relationships through performance records and results, and to shape the future together with them.

Learning from the Experiences of Others
In this book, I will attempt to vividly explain through personal experiences or experiences that have happened to acquaintances or colleagues, what lessons and conclusions can be drawn from them. A golden rule is that one should not only learn from one's own failed projects, but as much as possible from the failed projects and experiences of others. This saves a lot of money and time.

Declaration of War
You are in a permanent competitive situation, whether you like it or not. Not a day goes by, whether in club sports, kindergarten, school, training, starting a business, taking up an employment relationship or aiming to climb the ladder within an organization, where you are in direct competition with others who also want this. But the spots for this are limited or, what is even harder, in competition with yourself. And it is much harder to push, drive and motivate yourself than to do this externally. You are essentially fighting a two-front war, on one side with the outside world and on the other side with the inner world. Stop baking small rolls, pull yourself together, create your big fixed star as a goal and go full throttle from now on. You can do it, and you will do it. The same consistent approach applies to achieving small goals.

1.1 Success Means Growing Like a Tree

Once you have achieved your first successes on the way to your fixed star, you have completed demonstrable performance packages for yourself, and this in turn serves as motivation for the next work packages. This can be compared to a tree that grows, starts small and gets bigger over time. And the bigger the tree gets, the more resistant it becomes. This means that successes build on each other like building blocks, and the more often you experience success and have successfully completed demonstrable work packages, the more confidence and enthusiasm you will bring to the next projects. The nice thing about the comparison with the tree is that there is the widely branched root system, which anchors the tree very robustly in the foundation—by the way, there are very interesting scientific research results on how the long roots of trees in forests interact with each other—the trunk, the branches, the bark provide resistance. Ultimately, the tree is able to implement the best possible for growth and preservation in good weather (sun), bad weather (rain, snow), at different temperatures and under the influence of animals and insects. Everything started as a very small plant and the tree never doubted its growth from its nature.

You then set higher requirements for the next work packages, wider, higher, and more efficient, and with this training effect you get better each time. This requires that you always stay on it and do not give up in the middle. You will see that over time you will get better and better based on the work packages you deliver and you will also trust yourself more. The only one who can stop you is you. It's up to you, only you. I am always asked:

> **Tip**
>
> "Philipp, tell me, how do you manage all this? Your practices, your companies that you built and sold, your academic activities, your social commitment, and still always time to support other people, provide information and get involved?"

I reply to this: Nothing was created overnight. And it was not planned when I was a student, and that is now many years ago, that it would be executed in this way. But it was clear since school time where the journey would go with a constant learning and working attitude coupled with a strong will, and so it developed. There are recurring certain elements that have already differentiated during school time, looking back, from those who may not have made it so far or did not want to make more out of their life, the willingness to give everything until exhaustion. You also see it on TV with the athletes when they lie on the ground behind the finish line, regardless of their placement, gasping for air. In professional life, the willingness to exhaust oneself may seem strange, but in professional sports it was never different:

- **You are a professional, aren't you?**

On the other hand, I must say, I have never oriented myself to others, but have oriented myself to me and my own speed. According to the slogan "Demand and Promote" I demanded everything from myself and promoted myself accordingly by creating a fixed star, occasional reward and high self-esteem. If no one praises you, you have to praise yourself. It must always come honestly and from the heart. After a successfully and demonstrably delivered work package, you can speak some words of praise to yourself. As long as it is honest and corresponds to reality, why not? Self-motivation has never hurt.

It may have seemed from the outside that I wanted to outdo others or be better, but at the core, it was really about challenging myself, putting myself under pressure, and achieving the goals I set for myself. I wanted to rediscover and uncover my own potential, which can become an obsession or obsession when you realize over the years that you are achieving your goals and winning more victories. That is, most of the time I was actually busy with myself and not with my outside world, even if the outside world may have perceived it that way.

> **Tip**
> The most important thing is, you have to believe in yourself, there is no alternative.

There is also no reason not to believe in yourself. You don't believe that what others can do is not also within your potential. You either gave up too early or you simply don't believe that you are as powerful as all those you see where you might want to go yourself, or those you have as role models—you can cross that off directly.

> **Tip**
> You have the power, the potential, and should believe in yourself.
>   This is not negotiable!

Being successful simply also means realizing that you live a life that many others do not live. By this I mean that the lifestyle is somewhat different from those who do not want to achieve as much, do not want to realize their dreams or even lead a good life, but secretly long for higher goals that they apparently cannot achieve. It is absolutely okay to be satisfied with your life. No one should involuntarily chase after any goals or victories, but those who are hungry for victory and in a continuous "FIXED STAR-in-head mode" set themselves new goals and fight for victories, what is taken for granted in competitive sports, is demanded a lot.

> **Tip**
>
> First, you need to do an honest strength-weakness analysis for yourself and sensitize yourself to where your strengths and weaknesses lie. No one can do this better than you and it is homework you should do.

This does not necessarily mean that where you have your weaknesses, you do not become active, and it also does not mean that you have to remain where you have your strengths. But, you can write down, clearly, in detail and absolutely pure with yourself in conscience: Where am I good and where am I not so good?

Afterwards, you can make a **strategic decision**: do I build on my strengths, do I try to raise my weak sides to at least average, do I combine both, do I perhaps even have to improve one or the other weakness I have, no matter what the cost?

These are again strategic considerations. But the first homework is to draw an honest strength-weakness profile, and then you can decide depending on your fixed star: How do I design my commitment? Personally, I don't think much of saying after recording a personal strength-weakness profile that the resume is that I focus on my strengths, but the strength-weakness profile helps me to derive my work packages from it in relation to my self-chosen fixed star. And that can be, for example, if one of my weaknesses is sales strength or communication with third parties, or getting up on time or, or, or, that I have to take that into the boat to achieve my final goal. It's about creating a duty book, a task book to work off in the future and where you invest your energy and finances to build up competencies, skills and know-how.

Dealing with Pressure

You will have to deal with pressure on your way to your fixed star. Once with pressure from the outside world, situations that put your career or your business under stress, under pressure, and pressure from within yourself. That is, you have been working 60, 70, 80 hours a week for several weeks, you have little free time, get up early, go to bed late, some interim results are not as you had hoped, and yet you should endure it. In addition, there may be times when you are perhaps also suffering from a cold, getting headaches or other things are added on top, caused privately or professionally.

You must be able to deal with this pressure. And the best lesson to deal with pressure is simply to go through this phase. Like a nuclear-powered icebreaker. You can and will not be stopped by all these pressure situations! You should continue to drive yourself and go through this phase. The good news is that once you have such a phase behind you, you have the certainty that you can and will go through such a phase and will have the self-confidence in the next situation to also take this next phase. So there is an effect like an avalanche, it grows and grows and grows, you become bigger, you become stronger and more confident and can deal with more and more situations. Of course, it can happen that one or the other thing does not work in such a multi-week pressure phase. But here I always say, and you will read this again below, the 95-5 rule: Focus on the 95% that have worked, and do not carry the 5% that did not work out whiningly for months behind you like a crybaby. Always remember: Yes, the 5% that did not work out, you should analyze objectively neutral, consider what it was due to, and draw your lessons from it, but it's about the 95% that have worked! There is always a bit of shrinkage, in war one speaks of collateral damage, in other industries one speaks of daily form, and so there is some terminology in every area that tries to explain why one did not land at 100%. But I am of the opinion, and this has helped me in recent years, to focus on the 95% that I have successfully completed. I have taken note of the 5% and drawn my lessons from it, but I have never let it drag me down. Try it too.

1.2 The Best 10%

As you can see from (Fig. 1.1), you can tick as an exercise where you currently see yourself according to your own assessment.

Do you, in what you are currently doing professionally, belong to the best 10%, or are you at 11-25%? Do you belong to the group 26-50% or are you in the second half

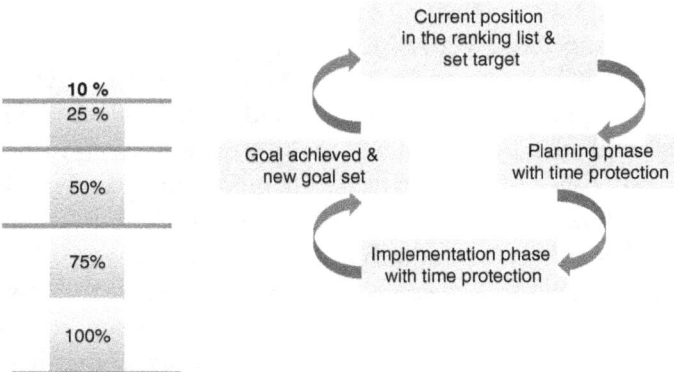

Fig. 1.1 "FIXED STAR Concept 2021" according to Plugmann (own illustration). The initial illustration describes the cycle of my concept for achieving self-set goals

at 51-100%? If you are currently going to school, then probably your grade average is decisive, if you see your activity in the sports club as a reference, then probably the question is, are you a regular player, occasional regular player or do you often sit on the bench, or are you possibly not even taken to the games? If you are in training, do you belong to the 10% of the best within your training class or are you rather in the percentile rank 11-25%, 26-50% or do you belong to the second half? And the same if you work as a journeyman/journeywoman or are employed, self-employed, compared to your competitors. You are better informed in your area than I am, but this is such a rough ballpark figure to get a feeling, where am I actually in terms of my performance, in the top 10% or not. And then you have to ask yourself:

- **Do I want to belong to the "Top 10%"?**

Am I already there, then congratulations, or am I not there yet and want to get there? Of course, you can also decide beforehand and say, I am satisfied with what I have achieved so far—then I wish you all the best. But if you are among those who want to be purposefully among the "top 25%" in your field or even among the "top 10%", then you have a lot ahead of you and I would like to help you with that. This reminds me of a nice story from my school days. It was in the tenth grade, until the ninth grade I was relatively lazy, studied very little, but always had C's and occasionally B's, and was satisfied with that, because actually meeting friends and physical activity interested me a lot and school not so much, and I always felt very comfortable that I was always somewhere between two and three with relatively little effort. Then, however, I found out that—I always wanted to do something in the health sector, help sick people, I also thought about working in nursing, so something where I have to do with people and where I can contribute to their health and well-being through my activity—and then I found out for the first time that with these grades, if I want to go to the medical faculty, for example, I would not get a study place. I didn't understand that at first, because I also didn't know what the admission requirements were, I was too young for that. But somehow my father made it clear to me that with this grade point average, which was 2.5 at the time, that with regard to admission to the medical faculty—where the grade point averages, around 1989, were somewhere between 1.2-1.7, I would have no chance. Then, of course, there was the medical test, with which you could gain some points. If you had, for example, a high school graduation average of 1.8 or 2.0, but you had a result in the medical test, which lasted all day, which was called the test best quota, I think it would have been the best 10%, then you got a better position in the ranking list based on a mixed calculation of the result of the medical test and your high school graduation grade. I also talked about this topic with my teachers, with whom I mostly had a good relationship, and they really confirmed it to me, they said "Philipp, if you want to become a doctor later, you definitely have to have a very good high school diploma, and also do a very good medical test". The medical test consisted of things like memorizing, reading texts and then reproducing them a little later, three-dimensional imagination, certain fine motor skills exercises of the letters b and q and p and the test lasted for several hours, I think, six or seven hours with a break. The problem was that in fact in the competition for this study admission you could not simply rely on your pure high school graduation grade, let's say 1.5, because the others who were also fighting for a study place also had the opportunity, by a significantly better medical test than others, to overtake these in the ranking list again. That means, it was a double requirement, first of all a one's high school graduation, as good as possible, and then also be among the best 10% in the medical test. So at that time, it was the ninth or tenth grade, I had a "wake-up effect" from one day to the next and had to think about how I could get to my goal from this "wishy-washy learning situation", a little learning and a lot of leisure time. So before I started thinking about how I could improve my performance, something fundamental had to happen. I had to somehow get myself out of my lethargy. That was very comfortable for me, I really did very little for school, and had relatively good grades, I considered a grade point average of 2.5 to be okay at that time. I could have easily studied other subjects that I found interesting, and I was at peace with myself. Good in school, I was also quite good in sports, and why should I exert myself so much? But since I decided at that time to go to the medical faculty, I had to change myself first. It took several months until a key experience happened, and I would like to tell you about it now:

At that time, I was in the tenth grade, I played in the school basketball team and in a basketball club in Cologne. We were about 20 teams, that was the C-youth at that time, and I was approached at a city championship game by a coach of the club BSC Saturn Cologne, the men's team played in the Basketball Bundesliga at that time, as far as I remember, BSC Saturn Cologne played with Bayer Leverkusen and Göttingen for the German championship, and I felt of course very honored that the youth coach of the C-youth of this club approached me and motivated me to switch. So I switched in the middle of the season, was not allowed to play a few games, and then, that was 1984/1985, the following happened, that the men's team became champion and was able to sign two Americans as players for the next European Cup season, and one of them became our youth coach. That was the transition from the C-youth to the B-youth, and in this phase I trained just as I had exerted myself in school, namely relatively leisure and fun oriented and always tried to implement the exercises that the coach gave us, more badly than right.

1.3 The New Coach

The new coach had no sense of humor when it came to training. He let nothing slide, absolutely nothing, I still hear his screams in my ear today. Every misbehavior had consequences. It started with punctuality. Training start, we had training two or three times a week from 5:00 PM, was exactly at 5:00 PM, which means, if you arrived at 5:01 PM, the hall was already locked from the inside and you could go home again, and if that happened a few times, then you couldn't play in the next game. In addition, there was a youth training session once a week after regular training in Cologne-Fühlingen, so it was a full program. This eventually led to us all waiting in front of the hall at 20 to five, sometimes even at half past four. The second thing was, we had to warm up, there was no getting around it, stretching and various exercises to get the musculoskeletal system into a supple, warmed-up position, and then training began. There were many different exercises, and during the first defense exercise, when you defend in basketball, you have to squat quite low, sometimes even stand on your tiptoes and then shuffle from left to right, and I always tried to have the tall center player in front of me during the exercises, so that the coach couldn't see me directly. This led to the whistle blowing in no time and me getting a clear dressing down. The coach, over 1.90 meters tall and a highly trained athlete, and I, the somewhat lazy point guard, stood opposite each other and he told me very clearly:

> *"We want to be successful as a team here and for us to be that, each individual has to reach their performance limit. If I believe in the success of the team and want to work hard for it, then I am warmly welcome, then he will give me everything he has in terms of know-how, skills and knowledge, so that I as part of the team contribute to the team's success. If I don't want that, then I should get dressed and go home and find a new team, there are plenty of fun club teams in the city after all."*

Interestingly, I immediately responded and said: *"Yes, I want."*

There was no need for long thought, and I was completely inflamed from one second to the next. I was somehow in constant combat mode, I was 15 at the time, and it continues to this day, over 35 years later, at this point, dear coach (my former teammates know the name), thank you very much for this clear dressing down. It was hard for me at the moment, but since then my learning and working attitude has changed significantly and was also part of the foundation on which I build today. I tell you this story because I simply want to show you that sometimes an **external impulse** is necessary to lead your own uncertainties and indecisions to a decision.

Because that is also a point, **you *must* make a decision**. If you look at the illustration, where you are in life right now, whether you belong to the "top 10%" in your professional, school, sports or training area, then you have to wrestle the decision from yourself, am I satisfied with my status quo or do I want to make more out of my life.

Because the idea that if you are now at rank 40%, that would be position No. 20 in a ranking of 50 people, you will outperform everyone later in the next performance section, i.e. after studying, after training, after founding a company, accepting a challenging employment relationship or implementing a private or professional project, with the same learning, working and behavioral approach that you have shown so far, is a utopia.

> **Tip**
> You should transform your mindset, this is your very personal compulsory exercise and nobody but you yourself are responsible for it! The future is not yet written, create your guiding star and it is up to you alone to shape it and actively work on it every day, through diligence, persistence, perseverance, endurance, punctuality, reliability and resilience. Even in digital times, these virtues or traditions have not changed to achieve long-term success.

Using (Fig. 1.2), you can do an exercise and mentally tune yourself to the self-chosen goals:

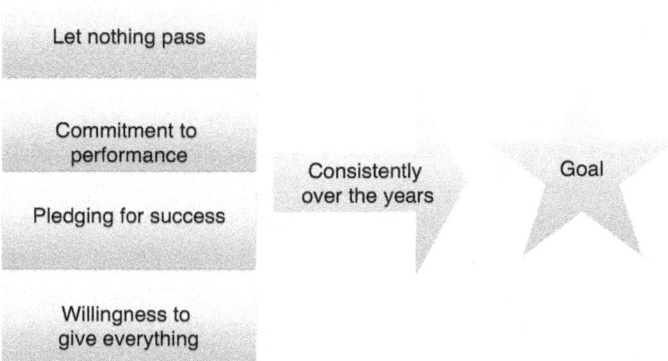

Fig. 1.2 "Relentlessness towards oneself" according to Plugmann (own illustration). This figure describes how you can mentally tune yourself to achieving the self-set goals

Of course, there are exceptions. I think of college dropouts, e.g. Bill Gates, who built a global company, but these examples are very rare and it would be bad advice to bet on being this one-in-a-million who messes up everything and still builds a world company. Of course, this can happen, but the aim of this book is to give you a toolkit to achieve it logically from your own strength and with a high probability.

1.4 The Written Form

I developed the habit during my school years, when I was confronted with the problem of having to transition from an average student to an excellent one, of writing down all current and future planning projects related to achieving a very good high school graduation average. To do this, I first took a blank sheet of paper and wrote down all the subjects, such as biology, mathematics, physics, sports, religion, art, social sciences, all the subjects I had at the time, then the names of the teachers, then the current written grades, the oral grades and the overall grades, and next to them the goals, the target grades, that I needed to achieve. Then there were simple things like, I was always good in sports and mathematics and biology as well. Those were the good performances. I was relatively mediocre in art, and then I had problems in English, for example, and occasional problems in two or three other subjects. So I had the subjects that were going well, the ones that were average and the ones that were going poorly. Of course, the big question was how to get better, where to start and what needs to change.

As a first measure, I spoke to the teachers in the subjects where I was not doing so well, telling them that I intended to improve, and I got some tips, it's no shame to ask for help or advice. Sure, it was uncomfortable, and I was a bit afraid of being laughed at. But if I seriously wanted to go from a 2.5 to a 1.5 as a graduation grade, the price was confronting the evaluators and myself, open communication and the willingness to bear the truth.

In the subjects where I was average, I also spoke to the teachers, asking how I could improve. In the subjects where I was good or very good, I didn't have big conversations with the teachers, and in the tenth grade I then went full throttle and always noted where I had improved, where I had deteriorated, kept track of the grades, and always had a **first-class overview** through the written documentation of the project. This helped me a lot.

At this point, I would like to remind you that you alone are responsible for creating and maintaining this first-class overview on a daily basis, this is part of the toolkit on the way to the fixed star. It guarantees you the ability to detect problems or deviations early on and, in combination with the individual time flow diagram presented later in this book, to shape the future—your future!

I still do this today, 35 years later, now digitally, but I create an Excel spreadsheet, write everything in that belongs to the project, all the points that are important, easy to overview, and always go in, in the evening, when I'm already in bed, I have my laptop nearby or my mobile phone, where I also have the files mirrored, then I take a quick look (30-60 seconds) and in the morning with my coffee I also look in and am always focused on the goal, the written documentation has helped me a lot. I would highly recommend this to you as well.

Write down your learning and work packages and projects so that you always have an overview. The idea that you could keep all this in your head and thus have an overview, I cannot share, because there are always small details added, and the overview, even of the details, in a very short time, to have everything at a glance in a few seconds, is simply worth its weight in gold, increases work efficiency and maintains motivation. Yes, you don't have to constantly re-think the tasks.

1.5 Mental Flexibility

Although I had everything written down, I had to realize at the end of the tenth grade that the final result was that I had stayed at the same level in the subjects where I was good or very good, in the subjects where I was average, I was able to improve for the most part, but I had three or four subjects where I had not been good for several years, and despite more effort and a lot of studying, I was not able to significantly improve my grades there. So, after the tenth grade, I had improved my overall average from 2.5 to 2.0, but that was the end of the line, and I had to make a decision. My mental flexibility helped me not to touch the fixed star, but to change the path to it, at least for a part of the way.

The question arose, since I already had the image of a poor student in the subjects I was not so good at, whether I should change schools. And since advanced courses were added from the eleventh grade, which have a higher weighting, and at the time of determining the high school graduation grade, and as far as I know even today, it did not matter which subjects were the advanced courses, I thought that I could take an advanced course in my best subjects, sports and mathematics, and since my teammates from the club were from a high school where a sports advanced course was likely to be established with a focus on basketball, I thought it would be a smart idea to change schools. And that's what I did. However, the sports advanced course did not materialize because at least twelve registrations would have been necessary, but only nine students registered for a sports advanced course, so no sports advanced course was established at all, and I ended up with mathematics and biology as advanced courses. Nevertheless, when changing schools, I had a fresh start, some students from other high schools also came, and it was like a restart, I did not have to deal with the image problems from the first high school, and immediately had an average grade of one, I mean, it was 1.6 at the end of the first semester of the eleventh grade. That means, already then I had to be flexible, I had my fixed star, my fixed star was a study place at the medical faculty, and the prerequisites were an excellent medical test and an excellent high school graduation, and to achieve this goal of an excellent high school graduation, a school change was necessary, I had to leave long-time school friends, also leave the familiar school environment, a new school, make new friendships, and I could not implement my original plan with sports as one of the two advanced courses, but you just have to stay flexible.

This flexibility, that you turn left, turn right, make a circle on the way to your fixed star, and continue somehow over a side path and stones, is part of it, but as long as you always see your fixed star on the horizon, you stay tense and focused, accept this and adapt to the situations. I believe that this element, in addition to the ability to deal with pressure, and also to constantly believe in and work on oneself and always have the will to improve, this mental flexibility and suppleness, to always deal positively with new situations, is part of it. You can plan a lot, there is also the saying "Man plans, God laughs." and that's how real life is.

You can plan as much as you want, life always brings new situations, and the fact how you deal with these situations and how you react to them, actually decides how you approach your fixed star. Because events happen again and again and some react very aggressively, very emotionally and very frustrated, others try to take note of it and then somehow deal with it professionally positively and make the best of it, like a growing tree, and move into the productive phase as quickly as possible, and sometimes it is also a training game.

I still catch myself reacting emotionally to bad news at first, but then calming down relatively quickly after a few minutes and trying to see the matter again soberly and objectively. Of course, there are disappointments, frustrations and setbacks, but everyone experiences them, at least I have not met any fellow students, entrepreneurs or athletes who have been in the sun for years. If you know someone like that, please call me, I have been looking for such people for decades.

This is like with all things a matter of training, you just have to practice, no master has fallen from the sky and if you are sensitive to such things, that you also have to learn this competence, how do I deal with bad news or with changes in plans, then you are prepared for the future.

Then the high school graduation was done, nice one-grade high school graduation, and then a few months after the high school graduation came the medical test, I could not yet feel safe that I have a study place, and was now in the preparations for the medical test. Of course, like all applicants, I first bought a practice book and informed myself about the structure of the test and what you need to be able to do, and then I found out that in these practice tests I did, I achieved a relatively average score. Then we asked around and the problem arose that it somehow became clear to me that the test does not really suit me and at that time the big question was, I recognized for myself the necessity to participate in two or three practice courses that were offered.

Each course cost 400 or 500 marks, and if I wanted to prepare for the courses as I had planned, I would have had to accumulate between 1200 and 1300 Deutsche Marks. My father, however, was not at all convinced and said that I should budget the money that was actually planned for a vacation with some good friends, because he thought that I was so good at school, it should not be a problem at all to pass this test well. But since this was a crucial criterion for the study place, I did not want to take any risks and negotiated a deal with my father. I just said that I would only go away with my friends for a week and then get the remaining amount for these courses. I also went to work, at that time I had a part-time job at a gas station, so I worked for it and also gave up part of my vacation. This brings us to the point of how determined you are to reach your fixed star. Achieving the fixed star will also be associated with acts of renunciation along the way. You will have to make decisions, do I spend money on A or B, and if A does not directly lead to the fixed star, perhaps renunciation is a good decision. You can then use the financial resources or the time resources to invest in your goal. But this is a standard exercise, it should be a minimum standard.

For me, it was worth it, I learned certain techniques in the courses, how I can solve certain tasks more efficiently, solve them faster, and how I can practice at home in self-study. Then, fortunately, I also achieved the top test score in the medical test, I mean, these were about the best 10% of the participants in the test, and from this combination of the top test score and the straight-A high school diploma, I finally got my desired study place. So that was the first phase, as I said, nothing is older than yesterday's success, and on the day of enrollment at the Medical Faculty of the University of Cologne, this fixed star was reached and it was time to look for a new fixed star. More on that later.

References

Althaber, A., Hess, J., & Pfahl, L. (2011). *Karriere mit Kind in der Wissenschaft: egalitärer Anspruch und tradierte Wirklichkeit der familiären Betreuungsarrangements von erfolgreichen Frauen und ihren Partnern* (pp. 83–116). Budrich.

Gündel, H., Glaser, J., & Angerer, P. (2014). *Arbeiten und gesund bleiben*. Springer.

Hancke, K., Toth, B., & Kreienberg, R. (2011). Umfrage: Karriere und Familie–unmöglich. *Dtsch Arztebl, 108*(41), 2148–2152.

Heinze, R. G., & Strünck, C. (2001). Freiwilliges soziales Engagement – Potenziale und Fördermöglichkeiten. In *Bürgerengagement in Deutschland* (pp. 233–253). VS Verlag.

Hitzenberger, J., & Schuett, S. (2016). Selbstwertschätzung: Professionelles Selbstbewusstsein. In *Mitarbeiterführung in Krippe, Kindergarten & Hort* (pp. 49–55). Springer.

Ihsen, S., Buschmeyer, A., & Skok, R. (2008). *„Ingenieurinnen und Ingenieure im Spannungsfeld zwischen Beruf, Karriere und Familie (VDI-Bericht)"*. Technische Universität, Fachgebiet Gender Studies in Ingenieurwissenschaften.

Kraaz, C. (2021). *Nachhaltig leistungsfähig bleiben: Praxis-Tipps für den Business-Marathon*. Springer.

Poulsen, I. (2006). Selbstwertschätzung und Selbstfürsorge. Burnoutprävention für Fachkräfte der Sozialen Arbeit. *Theorie und Praxis der Sozialen Arbeit, 2*, 59–64.

Rödl, M. (2010). Vereinbarkeit von Karriere und Familie als Teil der Unternehmensphilosophie der Wirtschaftskanzlei Rödl & Partner. In *Betriebliches Gesundheitsmanagement* (pp. 233–240). Gabler.

Rusconi, A., & Solga, H. (2011). *Gemeinsam Karriere machen: Die Verflechtung von Berufskarrieren und Familie in Akademikerpartnerschaften* (p. 191). Budrich.

Schulze, E. (2009). Stifterinnen und Stifter im deutschen Stiftungswesen. Eine Analyse der Motive, Ziele und Werte. In *Reichtum und Vermögen* (pp. 173–183). VS Verlag.

2

Transformation of the Mindset

The MINDSET of a person is defined differently. From an application-oriented perspective, for me, it is a mixture of personal attitude, the processing of one's own wealth of experience, and learning from the mistakes of others, self-motivation, discipline, and resilience. All of this is aligned with the materialization of the personal dream, the guiding star in the head, a strong indomitable will, sometimes even obsessed, regardless of the conditions, aimed at a strenuous long-term race, that is their MINDSET. The good news is, you can shape, influence, and change it. The MINDSET is dynamic and not a static, unalterable size. Let go of what was and focus all your strength on the future and your guiding star. Transform your mindset.

2.1 Attitude and Setting Goals

"How do you do that?"

In recent years, I have been asked this over and over again. My nephew, colleagues, and friends asked me, and eventually, I came to the conviction that I should summarize this compactly so that others can learn from my experiences and achieve their goals more efficiently. I am also aware that there are numerous different approaches and as different as they may appear, they can all lead to success in their own way. This guide reflects my views and recommendations.

At the age of 50, I have had many personal and professional experiences, achieved goals, missed goals, and this book is intended to help you set goals, achieve these goals, and never lose sight of your guiding star. There is tons of discussion material about success factors. Some approach it scientifically, with one side of the researchers viewing success factor research rather critically, while others consider it a fantastic tool. Basically, even outside of science, it is argued that someone who has been successful for a long time, and you ask what his success factors/criteria are, regardless of what really made the difference in reality, could tell you just about anything, because it cannot logically be refuted due to the success he has demonstrated. I understand that this criticism is acceptable. However, there are certain conditions, behavioral recommendations, and criteria that one can implement and follow, and which have a fairly high probability of leading someone personally to the goal, regardless of how others may have achieved their success. You can choose from the numerous methods and tools on offer, experiences and assessments, what suits you best, and there you and your decision are required. In the end, it is up to you to make decisions and live with the consequences. To make a good decision or to be able to make good decisions in general, you should have your own set of values, know yourself well, and only you alone can decide which approaches are most promising for you personally. This means that the very first task is, you can take the time and make the effort to think about who you are, what you can do, and what you want. And this homework is exactly what you need to do before you can benefit further from this book. I wish you a lot of fun. Please think about it: What are your values, who are you, what are you good at, and where do you want to go?

It is important to realize that there will be many defeats and setbacks on the long way to the goal, to the guiding star, to success. Some call it failure, others call it mistakes, others still call it fateful encounters. Whatever the name, you must realize that you can primarily learn from it. When deciding what your personal guiding star is, you must always realize that you have to choose between a self-determined or externally determined life. Also, the aspect of being able to freely decide from the rights and duties of our Basic Law and the democratic-liberal conditions, how you can develop your own private and professional life in any conceivable direction, should instill strong confidence and positive energy in you. All paths are possible and you lay the foundation for this through an uncompromising learning and working attitude over many years.

In summary, this means that when choosing your guiding star, you always have to consider: Is this what I want or is it a goal that is being imposed on me from the outside? It may also be that an externally suggested goal such as taking over a family business or a certain training direction appeals to you very much and you still have the freedom to shape the path and the implementation of this path and its effect on your future yourself. This should be understood as a great opportunity and the possibilities in our society should be used positively and actively.

Of course, such decisions also involve having the courage and the will to make your own way, and at some point, you will have to make a decision. There is the saying "Man plans, God laughs." and indeed, life is permeated with unpredictabilities, changes of mind, and events that cannot be foreseen. As long as you have your guiding star in sight, can rely on your uncompromising radical learning and working attitude, and maintain this macro view, you can deal with events at the micro level more relaxed. The big picture from the helicopter perspective gives one the feeling that the experiences and events of the present only seemingly lead one off the path, from the macro perspective they contribute to striving a little further towards the goal through experiences and learning from these experiences. It is said that life is a sum of many hundreds of decisions, and ultimately it is. You will always have a percentage of decisions that were negative in retrospect. But life is an interconnected entity and you must always view it positively, that everything has a benefit in relation to reaching the guiding star.

I recommend a weekly or bi-weekly routine exercise that lasts 30 minutes. I personally call it **"conceptual thinking"**. In this exercise, you retreat to a neutral place where you like to be on a weekly basis. This could be your apartment, a restaurant, a café, or you could drive somewhere in your car and park there for half an hour, and think about whether you are on track with your current activity towards your guiding star, whether your activities could be corrected, and try to reflect on whether your decisions are leading you towards your goal. In doing so, you always try to reflect on and think about yourself and your present. Always with the aim of positively influencing current and future decisions. The motivation for many people is different. Some strive for fame, others strive for an academic goal, others want to start their own business or contribute to the success of a company as an employee.

Whatever your professional goals are, whether it's overcoming mediocrity or turning away from boredom, always try to choose the goal that is in line with your individual nature. For this, you should take the time to consider: Who am I, what do I like to do and where do I want to go? Whatever your goal is, it is advisable to do the SWOT analysis mentioned earlier, a strengths-weaknesses profile of yourself, which opportunities, which risks you see in pursuing a goal, in order to get a better feel for who you are, what your values are, what is important to you privately and professionally, and what risks you will take on the way to your guiding star.

Despite the digital transformation of society and industry, core elements such as diligence (= hard work), determination, discipline, resilience, open-mindedness and perseverance have not changed as success factors ("virtues of success"). You must pursue your chosen guiding star with all determination and perseverance. On the way there, excuses are counterproductive. You must fully commit to this goal and bring about all the organizational conditions necessary for you to be successful. Only then will you be successful.

Using (Fig. 2.1), you can consider how to integrate your thought world and strategy into your own everyday reality:

It is important that you get into the habit of setting the next goal immediately after achieving a goal in order to maintain the tension.

2.2 Setting High Goals

I recently celebrated my 50th birthday and then had time in the following days to think about the last 50 years. Many of my friends and professional contacts kept asking

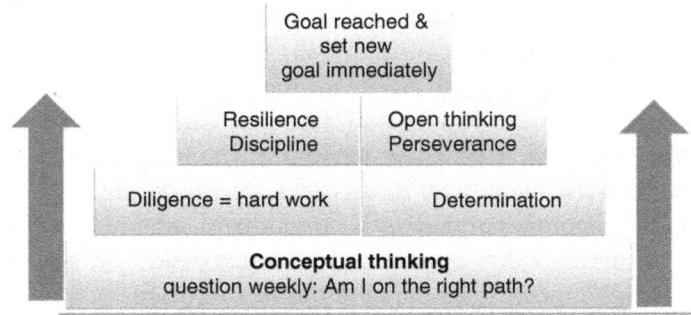

Fig. 2.1 "Concrete blocks as a foundation" according to Plugmann (own representation). This illustration describes how you can reach your goal in a modular way through conceptual thinking and the virtues of success

me: "Tell me, how do you actually do it? How do you manage all this?"

Since I kept hearing the question and asked myself why it is something special for the outside world when you go full throttle around the clock, I was motivated to create a guidebook to simply provide some practical tips and tricks on how to set goals and achieve them:

What are goals and how do you set goals?

If you now ask a top athlete how he set his goals, a top doctor, top painter, top butcher or a top mother or father, depending on whether the personal goals are small, medium or large, more in the professional or more in the private or in both areas, you always have to ask yourself in these success factor researches: Is the person who has set a certain goal for this goal low, medium or highly talented? Are the conditions and framework conditions favorable or unfavorable? Because it goes without saying that someone who has very good framework conditions, like many others, has not yet presented any results and has to go a long, strenuous, rocky path to achieve high goals. Proof still has to be provided, regardless of the starting situation, to want to go such a path and then to follow it permanently. Thus, the starting situation is secondary, the winner is recognized at the goal, not at the start. Let's say on the parents' side, from the social and financial framework or simply because he is blessed with a very good talent, or is it just someone who has an average talent, like many others.

> **Tip**
>
> I myself belong to the category of average talent, but I am a brutal work and learning machine.

I would like to bring this aspect closer to you in this book, among other things, because despite digital times, the conditions for being successful in the long term have not changed. I am very happy to repeat this until you can sing it in your sleep. These are diligence, discipline, reliability, commitment, resilience, and that over many, many years. Of course, there are ups and downs. I also have phases where I do less or lie lazily on the couch, but I have never lost sight of the goal, the fixed star on the horizon, where I want to go, never.

Surely you know the sayings from your youth: "Be satisfied with what you have," or "Who flies high can also sink deep." My God, what did one have to listen to as a teenager and sometimes even as a student. Later, during the company foundations, I got into the habit of listening and filtering out the positive.

It is simply important that you set a goal and stick to it regardless of the obstacles that come your way. In this book, I will repeatedly humorously conjure up old stories from the hat or tell experiences and simply report things that have happened to others, to visualize in the corresponding part of the book also the funny side of this path, which one has when pursuing a goal, and to give you some personal impressions of my path, which should simply show you that even with average talent, but brutal work performance and a very positive learning attitude, the goals are achieved in the long term.

One can realize that setting high goals, achieving them also always has a component of competition, because where you want to go, others want to go too. You are always in a competitive situation, be it admission for certain study places, be it a training place at a company that you find interesting, be it a partner you have fallen in love with, because you are not the only one. One should realize that life—whether we want it or not—is characterized by competition and that can be seen positively. It stimulates us, it makes us creative, aggressive, and one must detach oneself from the perspective that one could pursue a goal autarkically, but it is always a competitive situation. And that may sound strange to you, but sometimes you are in competition with yourself.

High goals are important because they have the effect of a magnet. The higher the goal, the stronger the pull. You know that you will not achieve this high goal in passing, and it will be difficult. This opens up your creativity, imagination, energy resources, and readiness to fight. It is important on the way to success to consider the sensitivities and sensitivity of the people with whom you interact. You must have an emotional antenna and feel what is possible and what is not. Because in part, the path to the fixed star also depends on who opens certain doors for you, offers opportunities, and makes an effort to bring you into contact with other interesting people.

I remember my first experience on the way to the fixed star and the feelings of people who influenced my career, as I slowly but surely began to bend, in the sense of I had to learn whether I proceed opportunistically or not. I heartily remember an experience with my then sports teacher in the 10th grade.

I must confess, I have a sometimes somewhat unusual sense of humor and our sports teacher at that time—surely still today, in case she is still active in this area—took sports so seriously that she did not tolerate humorous comments on the subject of sports. Of course, as a student with a quirky sense of humor, I was just right. So I always made comments like: "I also like sports, especially the sports show," and that led to the following experience at the Federal Youth Games: We had this 800-meter run and I came through the finish line at the same time with four other boys and girls and everyone got an A, except me. I got a B and in my somewhat cheeky way I went to the sports teacher a little later again and asked her (in private) to explain to me why I now have a B and the other four students, who also crossed the finish line at the same time as me, all have an A. Then she explained the grade to me as follows. As an introduction she said: "Philipp, that a student like you dares to question the grading of an adult teacher is already an impertinence."

Then she explained to me that the time was of course very good, but the running style was just a 3—and that together made a 2. When I told my father about it in the evening, he looked at me and said a two was also a good grade and I shouldn't be sad that the others were faster. I quickly learned not to provoke teachers, but rather to sway like a flag in the wind. That was the deal. Beating my math teacher in the 10th grade in the chess club, offering him a draw (politely) just before the end, which he declined and then beating him again, was not a smart idea. Always a solid 2, I slipped to 3 and no more discussions helped. One must pay attention to the feelings and sensitivities of one's fellow human beings and learn to estimate which words or actions will lead to which reactions. The decision is always up to oneself, whether one wants to reach one's fixed star efficiently or not. I exaggerated with the humor with my sports teacher, although she had said several times that she did not find it funny and challenged my math teacher in chess, without telling him beforehand that I played chess in a club and had already successfully competed in tournaments against significantly older players, some from the state league. If you intentionally or unintentionally emotionally hurt other people, you should not be surprised if there are feedbacks of an unwanted kind. On the way to the fixed star, it is therefore important to maintain etiquette and consider your fellow human beings. Moreover, it is also said that you would always meet at least twice in life and on a long journey to the fixed star you never know who will suddenly come around the corner again.

2.3 Self-motivation and Resilience

"What do you want to achieve in life, and how do you define success?"

The choice of questions is endless, at the core it's about what you really want to achieve deep down inside. Allow me to ask something provocative at this point:

- **Do you want to sink into mediocrity?**

The good news is that you live in a democratic society where you have the right to do nothing and also to do a lot. You can shape your lifestyle responsibly. This question has primarily nothing to do with finances. It's more about whether you aim to inspire people in a certain field of activity with outstanding products and services, whether as an employee, self-employed or combined. Do you want to have excellent expertise about the products and services in the field in which you are professionally active, to produce or develop such, and always to advance through innovation, creativity and empathy?

We live in a performance society, which causes stress and influences the everyday reality of the individual (by Kunhardt 2014). In this context, organizations, companies, institutions and individuals are in constant competition. Performance is based on experience and knowledge. Since the half-life of knowledge halves every 5–7 years depending on the field, you have to keep up. Further education and training every year, plus conferences, professional meetings and reading professional literature are minimum requirements to be better than the average in your field. Otherwise, you become interchangeable and have no distinguishing feature. This multiple burden of "working, learning, sleeping, working, learning, sleeping, working, learning, sleeping" over a long period of several months or years, leads to stress and pressure. Michalk (2019) describes in his book "Optimizing Health—Increasing Performance: Fit with Biochemistry" how you can turn the screws of performance with nutrition. Reif et al. (2018) help readers with tips for health promotion and stress management and Fuchs and Gerber (2018) show that sport can make a significant contribution to stress regulation. This shows you that you can have a positive influence on these individual factors, and thus you should develop a roadmap on how the individual areas can be optimized in turn. After that, you start to implement step by step and change your everyday reality. If a big hurdle comes your way over time, which may scare you or seem insurmountable, you have various options: give up or continue. At this point, you can shine through self-motivation and resilience.

Landes et al. (2021) describe the focus on self-motivation, that one can also contribute successfully and healthily in the home office with the support of self-motivation. Hennerfeind et al. (2020) show that self-motivation, self-criticism and motivation can be closely related and discuss that a leader has an advantage if she can motivate and inspire herself. Groß (2013) relates self-motivation and self-leadership in everyday professional life and points out that self-motivation also represents a piece of leadership work with regard to oneself.

This is thus associated with work and mental effort, to keep oneself on track and not to slacken in one's zeal and commitment. Self-motivation comes from your guiding star. Visualize your future with the power of your imagination and enjoy the idea of already having arrived in this future. The resilience, the endurance of fatigue, pressure and, for example, the adherence to deadlines or time pressure, no one can take away from you. That's your job, pull yourself together. For self-motivation and resilience, I use the thought technique of "negative reflection", as I at least call it for myself, i.e., I imagine that I would be one of those cancer patients with whom I often exchanged ideas as a young student, I would live in a country where I would not have access to education and health as in Germany or I would be trapped in a time loop from which I could not escape. This creates such fear and discomfort in me that I shudder and rejoice and am grateful that the conditions are okay and that I have the opportunity at all to go full throttle on my own. Everyone can do it differently, the imagination has no limits. But one can also make it clear that everything could be much worse and that it is almost a luxury to live in a society where one can simply shape one's future positively as one likes. That's great. What are you waiting for—step on the gas!

Lifelong learning is no longer a rarity these days and even after a longer break it's just a matter of practice. Hoffmann and Engelkamp (2016) show in the context of learning and memory psychology, recommendations to activate brain performance, Prenzel (1993) addresses issues of autonomy and motivation in adult learning and Kade and Seitter (2013) show possible educational worlds in adult education in connection with lifelong learning. The fact that one should learn to learn is known. It is recommended, especially in digital times, to take new paths to acquire information and knowledge and to bring it up to date. The element of autodidacticism plays an important role in this. I would like to tell you an anecdote about this:

In school, at the end of 9th grade during the summer holidays, I was motivated by my religion teacher to do a punishment assignment. My task was to conduct a tour of the church St. Maria im Kapitol near the Cologne Haymarket for our class after the big summer holidays. I was supposed to explain the differences in the architectural styles of Romanesque and Gothic churches and finally add some information about pre-Byzantine church architecture.

The frustration was great, because I had no idea about this topic. I started in the Cologne city library in the center of Cologne. When I asked the staff of the city library where I could read about church architecture, I already received the first critical looks. Then I was able to read a bit, but didn't get very far. So I decided to go to the church and sat down, it was nice, quiet, cool (very relaxing in summer) and I looked around, then I sat for a while and thought about what would probably happen if I didn't get any further with the assignment. The priest came and asked me how I was doing. I explained my problem to him and he offered to do a tour with me at a later date. This helped me a lot and after this tour I was able to think of further questions and ask friends. One of my friends had a father who was an architect, and he told me more. At the end of the summer holidays, I had enough information to design a presentation and a tour. The teacher was satisfied. And I had learned that with appropriate motivation and help, one can actually dive into many fields of knowledge, partly autodidactically. In any case, it took away my fear when starting from scratch in terms of knowledge. You should also not be afraid and practice the competence of autodidactic learning. You will be surprised what suddenly becomes possible and which worlds of knowledge will open up for you.

2.4 Good Conditions and Personal Dream

From my own experiences, I must confess, I also tend to complain about the conditions sometimes. If we are realistic, we are doing excellently here in Germany, globally considered. I had the privilege of having traveled a lot in the last 20 years. In Asia, the Middle East, Africa, North America, Europe too. And I come to the realization, every time when I came back and landed in Frankfurt, I was glad to be back in Germany. I can tell you some anecdotes about that. For example, when I was in Cape Town, South Africa in 2009 for a one-week training course, one quickly saw how things can go in some countries. For example, when you go to a doctor's office or a hospital there, there is not a sign on the wall with a crossed-out cell phone, i.e., that you should turn off your mobile phone, but there is a sign on the wall with a crossed-out revolver, i.e., that no firearms should be carried in the doctor's office. Many houses are fenced and barbed wire. But not just barbed wire as we know it, but really high-quality barbed wire constructions with barbs and cutting surfaces.

The crime rate in South Africa is enormous, and we were reminded daily that we could only visit certain institutions with security personnel at specific times and places. Looking at my first experience in San Francisco, when I left the hotel, I must say, I have never seen so many homeless people, beggars, and visibly impoverished individuals. I also think of the tent cities in the USA in recent years. Or simply now, for example, in India. The experiences in Mumbai with the open sewage system and the very different health system. If we consider the whole package for the entire population, we do not let anyone fall through the cracks here. We have a community system where we try not to let anyone slip through the net. And this is internationally outstanding. We can now see in the Corona crisis that our health system and our structures are stronger and more efficient compared to other European and other countries. And when we talk about achieving professional success, which is always connected with education and health, one must be capable and resilient, physically and mentally, and one must also have access to education. Our system here is such that, even if one had problems during school or has been working for a few years after completing an apprenticeship and is considering further development, studying while working, we have good conditions. Try studying in America without financial resources. Or there are countries where it's not about the performance, the potential, or the will of the candidates, but about how one is politically or socially engaged, what one does outside of the learning situation, which actually has nothing to do with learning itself.

Therefore, my personal experience is: We have optimal conditions here in Germany to achieve professional goals. It will never be perfect and it will never be satisfactory for everyone. But in the package, viewed from a societal perspective, the opportunities are available for many, based on my international experiences, and now it's up to you to make your decision and commit to having a specific goal and to push forward under these excellent conditions (compared internationally). I am already excited for you!

The Personal Dream—Never Give Up
The personal dream is something very intimate. It is your personal guiding star. In order to draw endless energy from this dream, you must keep the dream to yourself. That is the price. The dream consists of many small, medium, and large intermediate goals, but whatever your very personal dream is, you should keep it to yourself. Sometimes one wonders: "How big can my dream be?" And the answer is: "The bigger, the better."

The world of dreams is open and your imagination has no limits. As a teenager, I often heard things like: Boy, be realistic, boy, yes, that can be, dreamers fly high and fall deep. And standard statements like: You can't do it. And I liked best the people who didn't answer, but just laughed at me. Ultimately, it makes no sense to talk to outsiders, except perhaps with your family, about dreams, wishes, and goals, because whether your environment agrees with you or not, should have no influence on your activities and the ignition of your performance fire. Now is certainly a good time for an example.

I'll just tell you an example from my school days, which nicely visualizes the irrelevance of the evaluation by third parties, whether a dream, a wish, a goal is viewed positively or negatively by a third person. Back then in art class in the eleventh grade, at the new high school I had switched to, we had a task. We were supposed to creatively think about a desired topic and then implement it in an art project that has to do with social-critical statements. But we were free in the choice of the topic. Since I was playing basketball in a club in my free time, had a basketball at home and at the same time liked to be busy with model building and railway building in my free time, I simply took a basketball and painted it with continents and equipped it with various trees, mountains, and grass areas etc. and then also designed it with cotton wool and various colors, so that the basketball looked a bit like a planet, on which two, three factories work and dark clouds—the dark clouds stood for dirt etc.—fly around. And then during the presentation to the teacher, I dribbled the ball two or three times and then added, yes, we are playing with the future of our earth, and practically used this play on words "playing" and "playing with the future of the earth" and then looked at the teacher expectantly with wide open eyes.

What happened: The teacher stomped her feet and criticized me in front of the whole class. She had rarely experienced such a lazy student as me, it was not to be topped in lack of imagination and simplicity, I had made no effort at all to implement the tasks she had set. One could see that art is not for me at all, and I would be a deterrent example of how a student could be lazy and not even bother to hide it. Of course, I was devastated, got a four for this work and a few warm words on the way and of course walked around the schoolyard with my head down for the next few days because I was also reprimanded in front of the class.

As luck would have it, this teacher left the school for various reasons a few weeks later and we then got another teacher who did not look at this work anymore, but had a completely different approach. He told us, art and creativity live in every human being, every person can express themselves in a variety of ways artistically, creatively, craftily, literarily, music is also a part of it, and he is sure that everyone in the class, each in his own way, has something to communicate in the artistic-creative area. We should not be afraid, would all get good grades, and we would have all the freedom to express ourselves in the respective work as we wish. I must say, this basic art course, which I had until graduation, was filled with life, trust, confidence, communication, interaction, also between the students, and I am very grateful for this experience. That is, it was very nice to see how in one area an individual sees everything very critically, functions very energy-draining, quasi drains life energy and another in the same work field is completely different, activates people, motivates, gives joy and tries to respond individually to everyone. And I just tell you this experience from my school days because I was often able to make such experiences, in school, in earlier classes, in later classes, and also as an entrepreneur, as a student, and keep your personal dream to yourself. The dream cannot be big enough. Everything is possible, there is no limitation. Of course, you cannot currently overcome gravity and you cannot currently travel back and forth in time, these are physical conditions of the present. But how you shape your life, where you strive, whether privately or professionally, is your personal thing. Keep it to yourself, share it with your closest family members at most, and believe in it. You will see, with this dream as your secret treasure, you will always be able to see a fire in the dark, light in the dark, and draw energy from it.

Framework, Perseverance, and Self-Confidence

Framework conditions can shrink one's personal dream. One begins to reduce the original dream because one has experienced a defeat, failed an exam, or because a business year did not go well. My recommendation is, **giving up is forbidden**, because there is no reason to give up. There are always ups and downs. Switch from the micro to the macro perspective, try to see the big picture.

At 50 years old, I can look back and say: I have met more people who did not believe in me or who saw no prospects of success for certain projects than people who were positive. There are many explanations, practically speaking it does not matter why this is so. What is important is that there are the group of optimists and the pessimists. Some are reluctant to take risks, see everything very skeptically, are fearfully inclined and safety-oriented, and, when someone has taken a risk and failed, they mock the failures of this person or even want to add instructively, they saw it coming. Our society relies on people who take risks, who grow beyond themselves, who set goals and have dreams. Look around the world, everything you see has been created by the thoughts and actions of the dreamers around us. The people who stand by your side with negative thinking (whom you should get rid of as quickly as possible, if possible) also do not take responsibility for radiating negative energy towards you. And they also do not take responsibility if you ultimately implement and achieve your goals and dreams. It is simply an opinion that floats around in the air, and therefore you should get used to asking fewer and fewer questions about whether someone believes in you. You can ask factual questions, strategy questions, exchange experiences. But you don't need an approval notice from a third person "you have the potential, this could work". Get used to this right away. Trust in yourself and always have a healthy self-confidence.

Self-confidence is a special topic. Some children have it from the outset, some have a very strong self-confidence despite very adverse social framework conditions, others have a weakly pronounced self-confidence, although they have ideal framework conditions. It is hard to say how one comes to a solid, strong self-confidence. My personal experience is, one must believe in oneself and reinforce this belief through continuous hard work, learning, and commitment. Life is a long-term race, achieving dreams is achieved by some at an early age, others only very late in life. None of this matters, because it is your very personal adventure journey.

2.5 Long-Term Race

On the way to your professional success, you are in a long-term race. A long-term race is something different for everyone. For one person, it is a journey of a few years, as is known from start-ups, two, three, five years, for others it is ten to fifteen years, building a company, establishing a customer base and then selling it on, and for others, the long-term race lasts several decades. The term long-term race can also have different perspectives. Some may say it starts as early as the sixth, seventh, eighth grade or in high school, it starts with the application for an apprenticeship or with a part-time study, and others say, for me the race starts with the founding of my business, with the establishment of my practice, my company or the employment contract in my first, second or third company as an employee. Across all variants, this still means that one holds on to one's big goal, one's vision, one's guiding star for many years and decades. A good example, which is also often used and fits well here, is Elon Musk. One might have thought that he could have achieved his goals after his first or second company sale, but, as you can see, he continues, he enjoys it, and what his personal guiding star is, we will see over the years, as it materializes and becomes visible, which other companies, technologies and new processes, procedures, perspectives and activities open up.

The following aspects will help you in your personal long-term race:

Have the Long Breath

It goes without saying that on such a long journey of ten, fifteen or twenty-five to thirty years, many problems will arise. This is quite natural and is in the nature of things. One is not detached from the world, one has family, friends, personal health concerns and one is confronted daily, weekly, monthly, yearly with various events. The question is how one deals with these events. One person deals with it negatively, lets himself be dragged down and perhaps deviates from his guiding star or his intermediate goal, and the other tries to see it in such a way that he is grateful for the experience, draws his lessons from this experience and whips forward with the new insight. So, especially on such a long journey, you have to get used to evaluating more and more positively than negatively.

Stay Flexible

Easier said than done, but staying flexible means almost chameleon-like smoothly, agilely, actively and quickly adapting to new situations and constantly reminding oneself that this is part of the long journey to the guiding star.

Celebrating Intermediate Goals

It is important to also celebrate intermediate goals. By celebrating, I do not mean getting senselessly drunk or doing things you would not normally do, but rather, while striving for the intermediate goal, you already agree with yourself that when I have achieved this intermediate goal, then I will visit the cinema, go out for pizza with friends, treat myself to a day of wellness vacation, or do absolutely nothing for two days. However you design it, you know yourself better than anyone else, try to equip intermediate goals with rewards. This has the pleasant advantage that you do something good for yourself, that you deal mindfully and positively with yourself, and after a period of effort, you also do something good for yourself. This is important for morale and it is also a good performance reward principle to bring about positive energy with this goal again and again.

Going Full Throttle
Just like on a long highway stretch, you should step on the gas to reach your goal. This means, of course, you can take breaks, catch your breath, look around, but the principle always applies, step on the gas. And the nice thing is, while there is usually a speed limit on the highway, there are of course physical and biological limitations in real life, possibly cognitive limitations, but, to stay on the gas pedal for many years and continuously add a briquette year after year, to be diligent, to protect your time, and to always work on the next goal, pays off over a long distance. Because then you reach your goal.

Expanding Competitive Advantage
Long-term success means securing advantages: Since you are in competition with other individuals and organizations, the delta, the difference between the time and performance that you have available for your goals and for reaching the fixed star, is small in the first years. But as you can see from the figure (Fig. 2.2), the distances become larger and larger over the years and finally reach the point of uncatchability. You can secure a competitive advantage that you have built up over ten, fifteen years, i.e., the competition can hardly take this lead from you. Anyone who wants to set out to catch up with you must be willing to

Fig. 2.2 "Long-term race means full-throttle mentality" according to Plugmann (own illustration). This figure describes not taking your foot off the gas in a long-distance car race. You should never use the intermediate goals as a reason to idle, go full throttle

take on the time, the performance, and possibly the costs that are contained in this competitive advantage in order to reach you. And then the question is, are the competitive conditions currently such that, quasi ten to fifteen years later, this person can achieve the same success as you with the same costs and resource use. Because possibly the market conditions or the conditions for this person have changed in such a way that you are uncatchable. The delta is enormous.

Making Efforts
One of the core elements is, you have to make a damn effort. To achieve a superior goal in the competitive environment, a permanent effort is required. Just like an athlete of a top team at the end of the season in the quarterfinals, semifinals, finals of his sport gives his all and collapses exhausted, exhausted and satisfied, having given everything, you too must protect your time year after year, have made your plan, and then—and this is the strenuous part—implement it. Planning on paper is one thing, implementing it is another. And efforts are just strenuous, there is no sugarcoating there.

Using Fig. 2.2 as an example, you can see that many intermediate goals lead to the main goal, your fixed star.

The path to it is a long-term race and requires a full-throttle mentality, where you should not idle:

References

Fuchs, R., & Gerber, M. (Eds.). (2018). *Handbuch Stressregulation und Sport*. Springer.

Groß, M. (2013). Jeder Tag bietet eine Chance – Selbstmotivation und Selbstführung im Berufsalltag. In *Selbstcoaching* (pp. 123–127). Springer.

Hennerfeind, P., Hennerfeind, B., & Swoboda, R. (2020). Selbstmotivation, Selbstkritik und Reflexion. In *Soziale Aspekte der Führung* (pp. 31–38). Springer.

Hoffmann, J., & Engelkamp, J. (2016). *Lern-und Gedächtnispsychologie*. Springer.

Kade, J., & Seitter, W. (2013). *Lebenslanges Lernen. Mögliche Bildungswelten: Erwachsenenbildung, Biographie und Alltag* (Bd. 10). Springer.

von Kunhardt, G. (2014). Welchen Einfluss hat die Leistungsgesellschaft auf die Entstehung von Stress? In *Ein Leben lang leben* (pp. 117–132). Springer Spektrum.

Landes, M., Steiner, E., Utz, T., & Wittmann, R. (2021). Selbstmotivation. In *Erfolgreich und gesund im Homeoffice arbeiten* (pp. 9–14). Springer Gabler.

Michalk, C. (2019). *Gesundheit optimieren – Leistungsfähigkeit steigern: Fit mit Biochemie*. Springer.

Prenzel, M. (1993). Autonomie und Motivation im Lernen Erwachsener. *Zeitschrift für Pädagogik, 39*(2), 239–253.

Reif, J., Spieß, E., & Stadler, P. (2018). *Effektiver Umgang mit Stress* (vol. 8). Springer.

3

Time

The greatest asset you have is your personal time. If you sometimes wonder why other people manage to accomplish many things in a relatively short period of time, and it appears from the outside as if they have a twin because they are working on so many projects simultaneously, and doing so successfully, then it is simply because these people have trained themselves over the years to protect their time, to organize themselves in such a way that they can use their time strategically well, and within this time frame, to do and implement the things they have set out to do.

So there is a multi-step approach:

1. Time protection,
2. Time planning and
3. Time implementation.

You can imagine that within my private and professional environment, the funniest sentence I can hear is: "I don't have time." When I hear "I don't have time" in connection with a private or professional appointment or a project, it's the same as saying "I don't have money, I don't have interest." That is, it's actually just a pretext. But I'll go into that in more detail later. It's your time!

3.1 Time Protection—the Golden Weekend

Let's now come to the first point: time protection. What is meant by time protection? The term could be somewhat misleading, as one might think that time protection has something to do with protecting oneself or one's time from third parties, but it is primarily important that you protect your time from yourself first.

If you have defined a goal that you want to achieve, and are willing to do everything humanly possible and of course legitimate to achieve it, you can check your time resource as a basic foundation. What do you spend your time on and what do you use your time for? If you have set a goal that you absolutely want to achieve, then you should realize that the week does not have five days, but seven. When I was an assistant dentist, right after the state examination at the University of Cologne, I always considered the weekends as paid short vacations. I had Friday afternoon off, around 4 pm, and from then until Monday morning I had a paid short vacation. This is an important building block to realize that you should use all seven days to achieve your goal, and to abandon the idea and attitude that the week has five days, and that you can put your feet up for two days. This is not the case at all. You also need to realize that there are 52 weekends, and that means that if we now say 50 weekends times two days, we are talking about a theoretical time potential for you personally of 100 days. 100 days of doing or not doing, 100 days of learning or not learning, 100 days of physical activity or not, and that is the time potential that you can take into account from the outset.

Using Time Efficiently
If one of your goals is related to education or the acquisition of knowledge, e.g., if you are in training or want to pursue a part-time study, then Saturday and Sunday mornings are particularly valuable. Why? When you sleep in and/or wake up, you are usually mentally sharper in the morning hours. This means that these hours in the first third of the day from 08:00 to 14:00 are the times when you are simply fresh in the head, where you still have the energy from sleep, from the night, and you should plan your day so that you learn, read or recap something in these five to six hours, instead of spending the day getting up, going shopping, meeting friends, and then, on Saturday around 17:00 or 18:00, trying to do a learning exercise with all your might. This means, there is absolutely nothing wrong with having high goals and still having time for shopping, time for the family, for friends, for leisure activities, but throughout the day you should make sure that you use the first 6 hours of the day for learning. And if you then notice, okay, now I'm out of steam, now I need a break, exactly at this time, when you need a break anyway, go shopping or do other things, refuel, wash the car, go jogging, visit family, and then after a two to three hour break you can sit back at the desk, continue reading, continue learning and then continue the other things like interaction with friends, time for the partner, family, whatever, after this second session of 1–2 hours. With this process, you have gained about 7.5 hours per day and thus

15 hours per weekend, 60 hours per month, equivalent to 700 hours per year, despite leisure and sports activities, a huge competitive advantage.

This is, for example, a **daily schedule** that I have been making for myself for years, of course there were justified exceptions. You need to know best for yourself when during the day you can read/learn particularly well, when you have your peace, it may be that due to family or professional reasons or simply individually it is completely different for you, that you prefer to get up in the morning and do everything for the household, are out with the family, and then, when the children take a nap, then have 1–2 hours of possible time. Whatever your individual **daily time design** looks like, you can definitely take care of it and make decisions. Spending the day unplanned, as it happens, means giving up leadership. If you want to achieve your professional goals, you can take the lead yourself. This means, you should determine the daily plans yourself and not leave it to chance.

Acceptance in the Circle of Friends and Family

It is important that once you have made a rough time allocation for Saturday and Sunday, individual deviations are always possible and it can always happen that you are invited somewhere at short notice or are sick, or simply don't feel like it, it is important to seek acceptance in the family and circle of friends. There is nothing worse than setting out to achieve your goals and finding out along the way that your family or friends do not accept this approach, for whatever reasons. Often, in my view, a reason for this is a lack of communication in advance. Explain to your family, your partner, your friends, what professional goal you are pursuing in the next few years, what you plan to do and how you want to allocate and use your time and ask for support and acceptance. Say, you already know that there will be some weekends where you should decline, where you will not be there if there is something to celebrate, although you always plan in such a way that you can very well participate in barbecues, birthday parties and other celebrations. But ask for the support of your family and circle of friends and ask for understanding in advance if you should not be able to commit or if you cannot keep an appointment, for whatever reasons. It is much easier to get people on board and ask for understanding and support. People feel like they are part of this project and are positive about it from the start. This supports you later in exam phases or when you have to present something and are under time pressure yourself. And you should also point out that if you are short on the phone or do not respond to an email immediately, it may be because you are in an exam or stress phase. This preventive, prior communication in the family and circle of friends can be an important building block to receive support from this circle later in the implementation phase and to be successful.

Priorities

Another way to extend one's theoretical time potential is to get up an hour earlier than usual in the morning. Of course, this is challenging for a person who already gets up at 06:00, to then get up at 05:00. But, if you consider getting up an hour earlier than usual, you naturally also have to realize that you should go to bed an hour earlier the night before if you need a certain **sleep time quota**. So, if you usually go to bed at 23:00 and then get up at 06:00, then if you want to get up an hour earlier the next morning and want and need the same time quota, you will have to go to bed an hour earlier. Now you can say "but a nice movie starts at 22:00, or a football game starts, or I'm still on social media"—you should prioritize what you want. Do you want to watch TV or do you want professional success?

> **Tip**
>
> **To achieve professional success, you must be relentlessly disciplined.**

There is no room for discussion. Many people want to be professionally successful, but do not want to experience the consequences, the renunciation, and the hard, long-term work commitment. You can be sure, even if you are alone at your desk or in your car, you are in direct, tough competition with other companies, other people, for good jobs in the company or as a self-employed person in direct competition with other companies for customers and customer orders. Everyone is making an effort, everyone wants success, and in this tough competition, you must remain disciplined for your own good and the good of your organization. Of course, there are always setbacks, you may have a week when things just don't go so well, you are tired or sick. But fundamentally, you must not lose sight of your guiding star, which means sticking to it and disciplining yourself. There is no excuse, after a day when you had a slump, to say the next day, well, then I just had a slump the last day, and it all doesn't work out. You should motivate yourself, pull yourself together, and step on the gas.

Setting priorities can be a very effective organizational measure. Seiwert (2012) highlights the increase in efficiency that occurs when the number of activities is limited and focus is increased. Rusch (2019) describes how stress management and priority setting interact, with intense stress arising from lack of goal setting, lack of priority setting, and indecision.

Böttger et al. (2019) describe in the context of time management, that considering various behavioral dimensions of time management, setting priorities is inevitable, also to keep the stress level in balance and to direct the energy towards achieving goals.

Covey et al. (2014) describe in their book "The Way to the Essential: The Classic of Time Management" the advantages of focusing and setting priorities in order to concentrate on the essentials and to filter out background noise.

Quernheim (2018) shows how planning, whether daily or weekly planning, supports systematic priority setting and contributes to achieving goals. He emphasizes that the individual should take responsibility for his life planning.

Däfler (2018) deals with the application of time management methods and holds lack of priority setting responsible for constant stress. He brings the issue of digital transformation into focus, where numerous unread emails, digital sticky notes, and novel project planning applications bring new dynamics into the working world and can lead the individual into a state of permanent stress.

You can see from the scientific literature presented as an example that, regardless of whether you are employed or self-employed, consistent, appropriate, and well-thought-out time organization and priority setting can lead to the achievement of your goals.

Based on the measures listed by (Fig. 3.1), you can train daily to better protect your time:

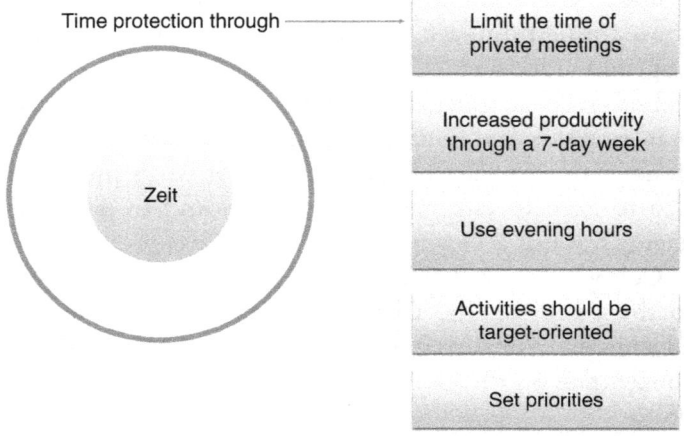

Fig. 3.1 "Time protection" according to Plugmann (own illustration). This figure describes which measures can be useful to protect your time

3.2 Activate the Time Saw

Time is your greatest asset, and that's good news, because you have free control over this "asset". The motto "constant dripping wears away the stone" can be rephrased in the context of this long-term race to say that with the factor of time you can achieve a high efficiency of impact if you work tirelessly towards achieving your set goals over a long period of time. For this, you should "activate the time saw".

Now it gets tough and it's up to you to make the following decisions. You have to start cutting out time wasters. Before you can do this, you need a personal priority list: **RECOMMENDATION FOR ACTION.**

1. Which activities lead me directly to the goal I have set?
   These activities are priority level 1.
2. Which activities directly or indirectly support priority level 1?
   These activities are priority level 2.
3. Which activities promote my health and financial stability?
   These activities are priority level 3.

Everything (in an appropriate style) that is not on this list must be eliminated.

Example

If I have set a goal, e.g. to complete further training with a good grade, a sales target, sales figures or a sports goal, I look at what is directly related to this goal.

Watching football games, going to the cinema or meeting friends for pizza on Saturday evening are nice leisure activities, but they have nothing to do with the goal. Shopping is necessary, but also has nothing to do with priority level 1. Sleeping in, hanging out ("chilling") or working in the garden are relaxing, but also have nothing directly to do with the goal. To make sure you understand me correctly, you will be able to pursue all these things if you want, but only AFTER creating the priority list and the resulting time schedule.

You can write on your priority level 1 list:

I. Time to read,
II. Time to think,
III. Time to understand,
IV. Time to memorize,
V. Time to exchange ideas with like-minded people.

> **You can write on your priority level 2 list:**
>
> I. Time to tidy up the desk.
> II. Time to learn about your own computer.
> III. Time to learn about work-easing software.
> IV. Time to learn about shopping services.
> V. Time for "conceptual thinking".
>
> **You can write on your priority level 3 list:**
>
> I. Time for a conversation with a financial advisor.
> II. Time for jogging.
> III. Time to check if I should switch from car to train for the next time to save financial resources.
> IV. Time to attend a cooking class (topic healthy eating).
> When formulating this priority list (levels 1–3), one might get the impression that much more time would be needed than is available. This feeling of time pressure is a good sign, it shows you that you are on the right path and now need to focus on raising time potentials.
> You are on a very good path—keep it up!

3.3 Innovation through the Individual Time Flow Diagram

One of my personal recipes for success is an individual time flow diagram. You have surely seen that when football or basketball coaches strategically prepare their team for the game, they draw and paint on a whiteboard, watch videos of the opponent, look at videos of the opponent's performance and strategy, but also of their own game variants, and visualize everything. The goal of a time flow diagram is similar. You are focused on the goal and want to create an overview from the starting point to the day you achieve the goal. It is important to write down the goal and record what the exact goal is, so you also know the point in time when you have achieved the goal.

> **Application Example**
>
> I would like to show you this principle based on the way I approach further education programs in which I have participated or am participating as a student. We live in a performance society where education and qualification are basic prerequisites for long-term professional success, in one's own company or as an employee, and therefore it is only logical that you participate once or several times in your career in multi-year internal company programs or further education offers from external service providers. These usually last two and a half to three years according to my experience and I approach them as follows: I always choose a calendar overview on the internet for the upcoming three years, which I can download for the next three years, then you simply enter "calendar" on Google, go to "images" and there you will find beautiful calendars that you can download and then integrate into a PowerPoint presentation or print out. And then you have, for example, the years 2022, 2023, and 2024. Then you lay these three printed DIN A4 sheets in landscape format next to each other on your desk and you know, for example, I am now doing a part-time bachelor's program or a master's or doctoral program, just like I do, I am currently in a part-time doctoral program, where I am completing my third doctoral thesis, and I did it exactly the same way. I took more time, you are allowed to study for several years, i.e. I internally planned for four years, but now let's stick to the three years. You now lay these three years next to each other, perhaps stick them together with adhesive tape at the top and bottom so that they do not slip, then take a few pens and different colored highlighters and write in everything that is coming up in these next 3 years. This starts with the presence times, the online webinars or online events. You draw in everything that is due there. Your birthdays, the birthdays of your partners, children, work colleagues, trade fairs, events, vacations, so that after working through these three years you have a colorful scribbled total overview of what all time commitments

are coming up in these three years. And, when my father once asked me—I have now also successfully completed three part-time master's programs—"Do you already know what you are doing this summer?", I told him: "I can tell you what I am doing in three years in the summer." Then he said: "Are you serious?" I said: "Yes, look here." I just showed him. I had these three years attached with tape on the side of my wardrobe and also showed him that I always update it when there is something to update, but of course I archive the old schedules in a folder. And so, every time I come home after a hard day's work, I immediately have an overview of where I am with just one glance. And when a module has been completed, then I cross it out, put a check mark on it, so that I always know exactly what is coming up through this individual time flow diagram. That means, as long as I have a total overview in relation to this goal that I am currently pursuing, whether it is a short-, medium- or long-term goal, as long as I have the overview, I cannot lose the overview. This is a form of individual multi-project management. And if I don't lose the overview, I also have no worries that I have overlooked something. I also see where a time phase is coming up where I have to do a lot of things in a compressed way, for example, you have to take exams in a part-time study program within a certain time interval, you have to prepare a term paper, maybe you have a certain project with a deadline in the company, and you have to pack all this into this multi-year overview. You will see in the end, it looks a bit chaotic, a lot of scribbling, a lot of brightly marked, and everything close together. If this is too chaotic for you, then you have to try to print out half-years. Then you have six half-years over three years, which you then stick under each other, there you can also write more, then you have an even better overview. You also have to write in buffers for vacation, in case you get sick, in case you don't get everything done on time. The art is actually to write in enough time buffers for all eventualities. So, of course, with increasing experience, it is possible to plan really tight, this reminds me of my wedding. We got married, the wedding party was in the evening and the next morning we got up at half past four because I had an event that I definitely had to attend at nine o'clock the next morning and in the evening we were sitting on the plane for our honeymoon. Tight fit, it's always a running gag in our family that we always do it like this, as long as there is still a second of time between activity one and two, it works. But you don't have to do it that extreme, but you have to try, and that's actually the art of it, because you know yourself best, to build in regeneration and emergency buffers in terms of time. And then it actually becomes even clearer on such a multi-year plan that you are actually already in the minus time.are. By the term "negative time", I mean that the time is already tighter in the planning phase than one would like. And you can already see that everything is going to be tight and scarce. It is also important to keep an eye on finances in the timeline diagram. It may be that after you have created this individual timeline, you suddenly get a feeling that, for example, hotel costs, travel costs, tuition fees, holiday costs, then perhaps a car purchase or some other obligation are pending; this can go in all possible directions. And then, based on this timeline, you may have to decide to cancel a holiday for a year and use these ten or fourteen days to study and advance certain learning or work projects, while at the same time saving the costs, which can amount to several thousand euros, that you would have incurred on a holiday, and thus also remain financially balanced. Such a timeline gives you a very good overview, you can determine where you spend a lot of time and where little, according to your priorities. Derived from this nice overview, you can then also decide on financial activities (transaction costs), where you want to direct certain expenses or non-expenses. In addition to this long-term overview over several months or years, it is also necessary to take a sheet and draw the days Monday, Tuesday, Wednesday, Thursday, Friday, Saturday and Sunday next to each other, draw the columns, and then also count the times from 00:00 in the morning to 24:00 in the evening in the column on the far left. And then you make a table where you have the times from top to bottom on the left, and the seven days as headings at the top. You can now draw a basic plan of how you ideally want to use the week for work and study. You then enter your working hours, if you are in an employment relationship, you are blocked from Monday morning to Friday afternoon, but then you have the time before getting up, which you can bring forward, if you always get up at quarter past six or half past six, you would have the potential to also get up at five or quarter to five, and in the evening, when you come home at seven, eat, relax,

> then you still have time from 21:30 to 00:30 in the morning for example, and the golden weekend, which is at your absolute disposal, and when I was an assistant dentist, I always saw the golden weekend as a paid short holiday, to squeeze out a total of up to 25 hours for study units. And you can do that too. You can get a weekly overview and see how you want to tap into the additional time potentials. And you should also document this and then also document when you have performed more, so that when you look back a few months later and don't really have a feeling, did I actually push hard or not, you can quickly regain an overview through personal documentation.

Decision Making

Now you have created this multi-year or multi-month overview, your personal timeline is set and you are in the phase where you are essentially reinventing yourself, a certain innovation process in the personal area, and this now also includes making radical decisions. Whenever one performs more, the issue of time pressure comes to light, and in order not to completely destroy oneself, certain things have to be cancelled or rearranged. This is a very personal matter and only you can decide. But it won't work without sacrifices, which means you will have to reduce certain activities in order to free up time for your goal-oriented activities. You may have to reduce certain holiday activities, and expenses are then also up for discussion. The nice thing is that everything now depends on your own decisions. Not others, third parties, neighbours or classmates or fellow students or competitors are your biggest problem, but your decisions and the consequences thereof. You have time to think, but ultimately it is only through the creation of the individual timeline and the weekly time overview that you are able to make sensible decisions. Decisions can also be adjusted, changed, revised with increasing experience, but the foundation of these decisions is always the total overview through a dynamic, flexible timeline, with the achievement of the goal you set yourself at the centre. Everything should be subordinate to this. The time and the personal financial structure. And then comes the implementation phase.

Implementation Phase
The implementation phase follows the planning phase and determines whether you will achieve a lot now or not. Since you now have a total overview of your time work packages—you have an overview of possible reserve time potentials and private and professional obligations—you need to know exactly what you have to do and what to achieve every morning when you wake up. So if you wake up on a Tuesday, go to work at the usual time and are back home at seven and you know that you still have to read, learn, work out or understand something concentrated for two and a half hours that day, then of course you are free in the evening to decide whether you come, make a coffee, and then sit down from half past seven to ten, or whether you first take a two-hour break and then sit down from quarter past nine to just before twelve. You can also sit down at eleven, do something until half past one, you can also split this time commitment, that you say, okay, that day I will do another one and a half hours, I can manage that, and the next day I had actually not planned anything, but I simply transfer this hour from today to tomorrow.

Or get up earlier tomorrow or whatever, you are completely free, but you always know exactly what you have to achieve that day and what your performance must be through the individual time flow diagram in the implementation phase.

When I then hear in such conversations, where I then tell entrepreneur friends or other people who were interested, that they set a big goal, that they then, for example, if it is such an educational goal, that they attend a program for three years, or further qualify or read up, that they create a multi-year time flow diagram, then also create a weekly time usage overview, and then go into the implementation phase, and then adjust and adapt daily and look and always look at their performance, and if they do nothing for three, four days, that they then adjust this plan again to make up for the lost time, then I hear things like "No thanks, that's totally stressful." or "Yes, it may work for you, but it's not for me." or "No, what's the stress?"

To that I can only say one thing:

> **Tip**
>
> **If you are not willing to set goals in the next few years, want to achieve these, and are willing to take the necessary measures, which always involve conflicts with yourself and your environment, which involve the elimination of activities, which involve discipline and effort, personal strain up to exhaustion, if you are not willing to fulfill these mandatory things, which you have written into your own work duty book, then you will always stay away from your goals, it will always remain just talk, and people will see from your achievements and results that you are not capable of achieving things.**

It is easy for people who have very favorable conditions, who are perhaps also gifted and talented, to downplay such schedules and discipline requirements. I can also tell you, I had a study friend who read a book once, he could still tell me half a year later on which page what stood. I always had to work hard for the knowledge, I had to read it, I had to mark it, I had to write it out, I had to partly memorize it, I had to make an incredibly high effort to keep up with the good ones, and in the end nobody was interested in who had what effort. He went on vacation with his parents for four weeks in Spain during the summer holidays and I then took a week off and used the other three weeks to study from morning to evening to keep up. Nobody is interested in how much effort you have to make to achieve a certain goal. **Therefore, in the performance- and result-driven society, only results count.** And, if you want to achieve goals, then you have to prepare yourself to move, you have to go full throttle and you have to positively engage in this competition with the environment and with yourself.

This is also a beautiful, creative process. One commits oneself to the performance society, one commits oneself to wanting to achieve something, and life is colorful. You can also say, I will go full throttle for the next five years and not do so much for the five years after that, and what I will do after that, I don't know yet today. That means, this is also a certain luxury in this democratic society that we have: Everyone can shape his life as he wants, as long as he obeys the laws and does not annoy others, that is wonderful. Look at other countries, what is sometimes going on there. We have a fantastic access to the education systems here in Germany, anyone who wants to can catch up on their high school diploma at evening school, we have various university options and the universities are also open in many courses of study. You can also accept longer study times at the universities if you have to work or start a start-up in between. Of course, life is unfair, that's clear, and some have it easy, others have it brutally hard, some grow up and have to take care of relatives or care cases, others have no problems etc. But especially there, I think, if you are not extremely talented and the conditions are unfavorable, you can just by applying an individual time flow diagram develop a very good overview for a goal and accordingly put the power on it. Try it out. I would be happy if you would share your experiences with the individual time flow diagram with me.

Feel free to email me, and if this strategy can help people, I would be very pleased to receive feedback. As always in life, there are a thousand ways to Rome. This is just one strategy, but I have been using this strategy since my school and university days; that's almost 30 years now, and ultimately I have to say that even in high school, starting with the eleventh grade, I always made these tables, these freely drawn tables, this grid where I incorporated the time, the exams, and the grades, and always had an overview of what was going on, even if there were bad results sometimes.

As long as you have an overview, you always know exactly where you are, and this leaves no room for wishful thinking, but you always know exactly where you stand. This is a good prerequisite for using your time and energy well. Good luck!

Using Fig. 3.2, you can get a complete overview of your time resources:

3.4 Hyperactivity

By hyperactivity, I do not mean a specific scientific term and I do not want to work through scientific definitions or terminologies here, but this is simply an expression that I use to describe how I act within a predetermined time unit set by myself and achieve as much as possible in, let's say, five hours of work, even without breaks. But it can also refer to a period of several weeks in which a certain work package has to be completed, regardless of how much other work comes in professional or private matters.

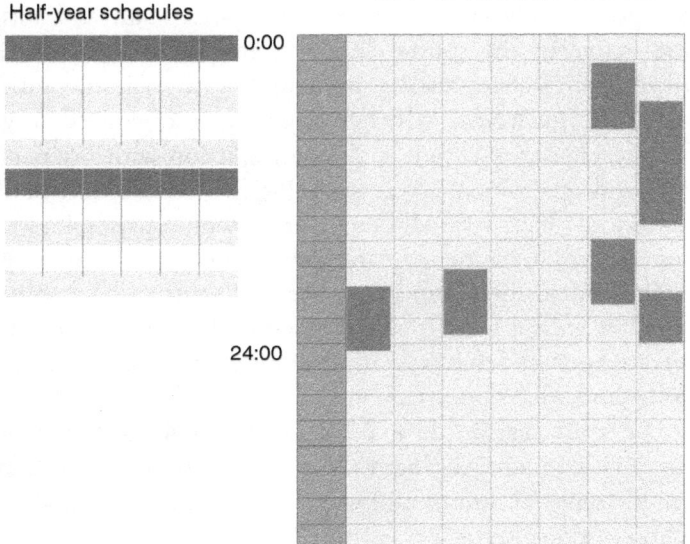

Fig. 3.2 "Time flow diagram" according to Plugmann (own representation). This figure describes how you can create an overview of your entire time

I like to compare this with artists, musicians, poets, creatives, who simply have a phase of several days or weeks where ideas are sprouting from them, where the joy of working and creating, the joy of design and materialization of ideas is so great that they forget time and space, and march through this time with relatively little sleep and a high energetic effort and lead the work package to its goal. This is of course always interesting when you are hyperactive in a certain environment, as I like to use the word, and the environment perceives this as deviating from the norm.

I can tell you a very nice anecdote from my school days. After I was very active in class in the tenth grade and also engaged socially, played in the club sports team and was also active in the sports club, was interested in art and asked my teachers about opportunities to visit the university or museums, whether anything is organized, my class teacher at that time had a conversation with my parents and recommended a psychological consultation or I should just have a casual conversation with a psychologist. Yes, and as it happened, one day I came home and my father said to me: "You know, we just want to bring you together with a person of trust, with whom you can talk for an hour about how you are doing and what you are doing and what concerns you."

For some reason, they didn't want to tell me that this was a visit to a psychologist. Now, of course, I have a very unique sense of humor and went there one afternoon after school. I don't know, I was 14 or 15.

He was a nice man, he introduced himself, said he coaches and advises family psychologically. And I thought to myself, because I remember it very well to this day, well, let's see what kind of show is going on now. And he said to me: "Yes, your parents are worried, and do you have any questions for me?"

I have a very peculiar sense of humor and asked him: "You probably want to tell me something about my disturbed father-son relationship or about bullying at school, right?" I was already out of favor with him. He told me that I was not taking the conversation seriously, and I said: "I see no need to talk about personal things with a complete stranger." And then he leaned back and said: "Ah, I see. That's the way the wind blows." So, we were already in confrontation after 60 seconds and as the conversation went on, we came to the point where I was reproachfully told that I was bringing stress and haste into the class by raising my hand too often, and that I was putting the teacher under pressure with my constant questioning. The teachers were stressed and the classmates were stressed and this—the word "hyperactivity" was used at the time—must have a cause. That means, as it often is, nobody cares about your individual situation, your individual goals, and the motivation and drive situation, but you are compared with average values, a standardized view of a group of people, in this case of school classes, and if one deviates too far from what is written as the so-called norm, then there is directly a conspicuousness. I don't even want to talk about the fact that they then also try to regulate this positive willingness and ability to perform, which is reflected in questions, in numerous activities and a positive performance perception, with medication.

Of course, this is the absolute horror and one simply has to be careful not to fall into disadvantages in a society of increasing acceptance of mediocrity, equality, and non-differentiation, because one exercises the right to perform more. As much as an anecdote and I simply have not forgotten this conversation, because I, of course, as a father, uncle, and friend of many friends who have children, always sensitize when I hear somewhere that someone who does a lot, even at a young age of 14, 15, 16, 17, is linguistically cornered, that more activity or, as I call it, hyperactivity is negatively evaluated in any form.

The prerequisite to be hyperactive over a period of several weeks is that you first create the conditions for yourself. This starts with small things like a clean desk, sufficient writing material, computers must be available, the tasks within this e.g. six weeks should only be limited to the mandatory working hours, outside of working hours, in the company or institution where you work, or in your company, you must protect the time extremely. The second is, you should turn off your mobile phone if possible and you should give your circle of friends and acquaintances and the family preventive information that you will be going full throttle for the next four or six weeks, so that the environment is also mentally prepared for it. The other thing is, you have to adjust your time in terms of the time resource so that you get up early in the morning and go to bed relatively late at night.

There are many strategies, people who say they get up at five or half past five or half past six, others who go to bed at one in the morning or two in the morning. This cannot be established as a universally valid principle. You can have a phase where you say, well, I'm going to get up at quarter to five or five every morning for the next three weeks and go to bed at eleven in the evening. Or you say, I get up as usual and go to bed at midnight. You have to prepare yourself to accept and endure a certain basic tiredness. Since this is limited in time to four to six weeks, this is my personal experience, you can also cope well with phases close to fatigue and exhaustion during this time. Such a hyperactive time period is very individual. I like to compare it to riding a wave. Although I am not a surfer myself, I simply imagine that you have this wave as a time period, and you yourself are the surfer, and you know yourself best. You have to put together your own individual package, how far can you endure tiredness over a period of several weeks, how far can you get up relatively early than usual, and it is also a kind of training matter. Once you have been running this program for a few weeks, you will also find that you don't fall over from it, after all, you are not made of sugar, you are resilient.

Other people on the planet live and reside under much more difficult conditions. We live here in a very safe and very comfortable environment and you have everything you need, food, drink, a roof over your head, the heating works, food is available around the clock, you can use online ordering services for clothing, utensils and food, mobility is secured in all variations and communication possibilities are also unrestricted. In this respect, you have optimal conditions for such a four- to six-week power phase. Then take several white sheets, maybe one sheet for each week, make columns and rows and write in what you have to achieve by when. For example, if I have a book project—this is currently my eighth book project—then I know when I have to submit to the publisher, I know how many pages I have to write, I need another four weeks at the end to read everything calmly. You usually let the work settle for one or two weeks, read a manuscript again, you have to let spelling, sentence structure, reading flow work again, possibly rearrange text modules because the reading flow is not guaranteed.

When you write a book over several months, you develop a certain operational blindness, and when you then, after letting the manuscript lie for a week or two, read it again, you think, oh, I must have taken a break there, or I missed something. That is, I write all this down. I also know how many pages need to be delivered, and I factor in that I might be sick for a week or have a headache or not feel like it, and then I make a schedule. And I transfer this schedule onto these white sheets, one sheet for each week, and stick them, for example, on the wardrobe. These are usually about eight to ten white sheets, which I have labeled either horizontally or vertically, and then I stick them on the wardrobe or on the back of my door with tape. Then it's time to hear the starting shot and then work through this. This written plan, of course, is also adjusted flexibly and dynamically, as they say, "on the flight", so for example, I surprisingly accomplish much more in one day, but then maybe I'm exhausted for two days, or I have to take a break for three or four days for personal reasons, then I distribute the lost time over the remaining days. And so I always adjust this plan. It is important that you archive these sheets, in a quick file or in a clear sleeve, and that you can review these completed work packages later, in later years, and also show yourself how you planned back then, how you always dynamically adjusted it, and that you indeed achieved the goal you set. And the more of these clear sleeves or folders with successfully completed work packages and achieved goals you have in front of you on your shelf, the more your self-confidence grows. The goals can then be expanded and redefined again and again, you also gain experience and get to know yourself better within this performance period.

Hyperactivity also means to me that you have a high work intensity within time units. We all know this, we sit down at the desk, I always say, the hardest sport in the world is to sit at a desk non-stop for a day with small food and toilet breaks. Try to sit down at the table at seven in the morning and go through until 11:00 p.m. with small breaks, maybe go jogging, lie down for a short while, but otherwise be at the desk 90% of the time, whether it's to write, learn or work on the computer. So that's also a sport in itself. Of course, you have to somehow banish the phone from your workplace for a few hours. The temptation to constantly check Facebook, LinkedIn, Instagram is enormous. You constantly receive messages via WhatsApp groups and other communication service providers, you constantly check in, you want to be a quick responder, to respond quickly, but it distracts from work. That means, you have to define a time for yourself, that you say, okay, I pull through from 08:00 to 13:00 in the morning, then I take a break from 13:00 to 15:00, I eat, lie down or go jogging or shopping, because I'm flat anyway, and then, during that time, I also check my messages. Then you work through again from 15:00 to 20:00 and then, after you have worked intensively for a total of ten hours that day, you can wonderfully sit in front of the evening news, watch football, meet friends, call a friend, do whatever you feel like. You can look back on the day and know that you have worked ten hours, and this also intensively.

When I say "highly intensive", I don't mean that you work hectically or excessively fast, but actually I mean the standard state, that you are fully concentrated on the task at hand during the time you are learning, working. And this actual normal standard is somehow referred to as hyperactive or hyperintensive today. From my experience, it's simply about being mentally present in the work or learning area with high concentration and not being distracted by other things. And this also includes telling your family that you would like to take out the trash, wash the car or take care of other things that day, but preferably within the time when you have set up fixed breaks. The optimal case is, of course, that this is possible. Of course, everyone has their individual lifestyle and everyday reality and it is not always possible. And therefore it is sometimes better, even if it is very early, to get up at four in the morning and, if it is a weekend or if it is a workday where it is possible, then to go full throttle for three, four hours, and then possibly to go to work a little later or to go to bed relatively late at night. So at 01:00 or 02:00 a.m., if you pull through completely from 10:00 p.m. to 02:00 a.m., then that's also possible.

I often hear, when I talk to friends or entrepreneurs about these things, that one gives full throttle for three to four hours in the evening during the week, that then it is said, the day was so long, and I am so exhausted, and I am so tired, and nothing productive comes out of it anymore. I have to say, you can't accept that, these are all excuses and justifications for not moving your butt. And you have to know what you want. If you want to achieve a goal that you have set and if this goal is important to you, and for your family, and for the future, then you have to make a pot of coffee, or you have to lie down for half an hour from half past nine to ten, and then you can give full concentration for another three to four hours. Then it is often said, what are these three or four hours supposed to bring? Well, the three to four hours in themselves, that's one thing, if you, for example, arrange your behavior so that you do this on Mondays, Wednesdays and Fridays, and then ten hours are added in the evening during the week, then that's 40 hours in the month, and then that's 120 hours in the quarter.

It does make a difference, let's just take the number 100 hours, Monday to Friday, if you simply have 100 hours more than competitors or compared to your own work power, than if you didn't have these 100 hours.

I don't even want to bring up the topic that you haven't even tried it yet. You're essentially admitting defeat before you've even started. And that's why it can rightly be called an excuse. **Give it a try.** Start with one evening a week, e.g. Monday evening, when you might still be a bit fresher from the weekend, and push hard again from half past nine to half past one and focus 100% on what you have in front of you, what you are learning or working on. Try this for two, three weeks and if it works, add Wednesday. If you've used Monday and Wednesday to gain another three to four hours, then try it out on Friday as well and if Friday doesn't fit, it's not a problem, you can also combine, you can also say Tuesday, Wednesday, Thursday or Tuesday and Thursday.

What's important is that you set it up individually and get to know yourself under stress, under fatigue and near exhaustion, and also develop a good physical and mental feeling for what is good for you and what is not. It's not about crossing red lines and if you're totally tired the next morning and can't do your work reliably, then still always follow this principle. It's about trying out, based on your personal stress potential, whether you can go from 75% stress to 90-95% stress for a certain period of time, for example six weeks. And no one can determine this better than you. **What's important is that everything stays healthy and that you don't overdo it extremely.** Because a line can also be crossed where it's simply too much. But, just like in sports, there's always room for improvement in your job and you just have to find out what your very personal work and learning style is to achieve the goal you've set.

Everyone has their tricks, I have my tricks too. I have traditionally made it a habit, after a four to six week power phase, where I'm really hyperactive, where I always get up earlier than I need to and go to bed later than I should, where I work on a work package and achieve the set goal, to reward myself after such a six week phase. This could be, for example, that I close the practice on a Friday, sleep in that day, then go to the cinema in the afternoon when most people are working, then it's an absolute luxury for me to sit in a relatively empty cinema, eat my popcorn and drink a diet coke. Then maybe I go out for some delicious food, go into town and buy myself a shirt and take a nap at home in the afternoon. Of course, all in consultation with the family. And I think, if you've given it your all for six weeks and delivered your work package, in whatever form, be it a work or learning goal, then you can also treat yourself to a day. And this reward principle doesn't have to be anything luxurious, but you consciously decide to take a day off. You should also keep this principle. See what's good for you, and if you've reached the goal after such a power phase, just treat yourself to a reward. You've earned it.

In addition, I would like to present to you aspects from the scientific literature that are exciting in the context of "hyperactivity". Goodman et al. (2000) show the challenges parents can have with hyperactive children, be it nocturnal awakening, naughtiness or dominance seeking, and analyze the term from the perspective of child psychiatrists (general motor restlessness, inattention). I find it interesting that both lack of impulse control/increased impulsivity and a "continuum of attention and activity of the general population" are discussed. Perhaps you now feel like me and a strange feeling comes over you. Not only children, but also adolescents, young adults and adults are compared with the "general population" on the topic of hyperactivity. This reminds me of the movie "George Orwell 1984". Are we all a mass? Is no individuality, also in terms of personal activity, desired? Can a school class no longer handle conspicuous students given the already overwhelmed school structures? At the end of the day, do we leave the field to those people who believe that only a certain behavior and activity intensity corridor can be tolerated when it comes to determining normality, mediocrity, otherness and freedom, the rights anchored in the Basic Law? Is the assumption correct that impulsivity, nocturnal restlessness or dominance seeking are negatively connotated? The English would say "It depends" and that's the crux of the matter. My personal experiences with psychologists and child psychiatrists in my youth were characterized by blame, behavioral guidelines and a lack of willingness to address individuality. These are open questions that can be discussed in a detailed discussion. As always, the truth probably lies somewhere in the middle.

Speaking for myself, I can say that I liked to study and write at night, sometimes I went to bed at 10 pm, then got up at 3, read or wrote something and went back to bed at 5 am. On Friday nights, I liked to paint, read, write or watch TV until the early morning and then sleep in. Occasionally, I didn't sleep at all at night and then went to bed earlier the next day. At night it is so quiet, the thoughts are clear and I could do something very concentrated, that was great. Everyone has their own way of organizing things, and I took that freedom. My parents were worried and through conversations with psychologists and child psychiatrists, I had a unique opportunity to experience the absurdity of reality on my own skin.

Summary

The core of success to be hyperactively active is:

1. Note the upcoming work and learning package.
2. Create temporal opportunities to work highly concentrated on what you have planned.
3. Test your personal stress limit, train and expand it, but always stay within a healthy measure and WITHOUT crossing the red line.
4. Reward yourself. You have earned it.
5. Nothing is older than yesterday's success. Now it's time to set the next goal after the reward. Good luck.

3.5 Designing the Network

You know the expression "contacts, contacts and more contacts". In the sales industry, the more contacts, the more contracts. Anyone who thinks they can do everything alone will be surprised. As I have already described in previous chapters, success is always a team effort. You are dependent on the cooperation or collaboration with other individuals or organizations, because you are never completely alone. In professional life, but also privately, there are, in a compact summary, some important core tasks that you should work on:

1. You should always involve your personal and professional circle in your efforts, whether it's training or further education. This means that you should communicate in your private environment that a multi-year period is now beginning, during which you will be completing further training with a specific goal.
2. The opinion of others, which is also a task that you need to train yourself to do, should ultimately be irrelevant. Of course, you can always take note of the opinions of third parties and assess to what extent there is a factual core to them, but everyone has the right to their opinion and you have just as much right to let it bounce off you.
3. Eliminate so-called "Toxic People" from your private and professional environment. The definition of "Toxic People" varies greatly. Essentially, it's about banishing people who constantly complain, whine, and shout about how terrible everything is from your environment, or reducing communication with these people to the bare minimum, because you have committed yourself to a performance philosophy. This means that you are capable and willing to perform, and want to gradually achieve the goals you have set. This means you need an environment that is also motivated, that communicates openly, exchanges experiences, and not only talks about successes, but also about failures, and so to speak, mutually benefits from the experiences and emotions of others and encourages each other to new peak performances over the months and years. Even when setbacks and disappointments occur. This is a so-called team spirit.

    Of course, if you have people who, instead of moving their butts, whine from morning till night and look for the last straw not to perform, and constantly save themselves, but rather talk about others for hours and

tear their mouths, then you have to exclude these people from your close private and professional circle. In this way, you create a circle of people who are positive towards you, who support you, who help you improve your weaknesses and build on your strengths, who promote you in good and bad times, believe in you and support you. And with this environment, you have the best prerequisites to successfully get through the next few years and to successfully achieve the goals you have set for yourself.
4. You often hear "Show me your network and I'll show you who you are" and now there are many different radical theses circulating on the internet that if you develop professionally, so to speak, if the delta to your circle of friends becomes large, you should detach yourself from this old circle of friends and then look for a new circle of friends.

I personally don't think much of this, because professional development automatically leads to you meeting new people and that in your work environment, through further training and certain projects and activities and increasing professional experience, you naturally come into contact with older and more experienced colleagues and thus your professional network is constantly evolving. In addition, you can build additional contacts through today's social media like LinkedIn, Xing and other digital communication possibilities. I actually see the so-called old circle of friends as the regeneration zone par excellence, because there you are loved and appreciated just as you are. They know you from your childhood and youth, they share the same dreams and experiences, one wanted to become an astronaut, another an artist, the third wanted to travel around the world, everyone has taken a different path in life, privately and professionally, everyone has had highs and lows, everyone has celebrated exuberant successes and gone through deepest failures, and there is actually nothing more beautiful than getting together with this old, long-standing, traditionally grown circle of friends.

There, people also know who you are and that keeps you grounded. Therefore, I don't think much of these radical theses that are often propagated on the internet. And ultimately, I would say that I would actually transform the saying into: "Show me your work and learning effort from last year and the work packages that you have completed, and I'll tell you where you'll be next year.". Because ultimately, at its core, you should always look at yourself and your own, very personal willingness to mutate into a learning and working machine, as I like to say, determines whether you achieve the goals you have set for yourself in the long term or not. And not whether you know three people here and two people there. And certainly not that you distance yourself from your long-standing friends in any way.

Designing the network also means a high time commitment and outstanding dedication. You have to make an effort and strive to attend certain trade fairs, certain meetings, gatherings, club activities, to accept invitations and use your time efficiently. So, if you receive an invitation to participate in a certain activity, which often takes place in the evenings during the week after the workday, then it depends on your personal decision whether you will seize the opportunity or not. If you talk yourself into a mental state where you say: "Oh God, the day was so long, I worked from 08:00 to 15:00, and then I only got home at 16:30, and then I'm supposed to go somewhere at 19:00 or 20:00.", then you can already say goodbye to your ambitions for success. I want to give you a comparison:

If a doctor in the hospital has a 24-hour shift, in which he works from eight in the morning until eight the next morning, with very short periods of rest, I'm not even talking about how intense the work is within these 24 hours during Corona times, when you work in the emergency room or in intensive care, all doctors work very dedicatedly and nobody would think of complaining, in comparison, if you work from 08:00 to 16:00, after eight hours and say: "Oh dear, I have now worked eight hours, how am I supposed to survive this?" You have to see it from the other perspective.

You don't need to pull a 24-hour shift. You are also not forced to pull an additional 24-hour shift twice a week, but you have a nine-or-ten-hour time unit. We humorously call this "Mickey Mouse working hours" in our professional environment. This is not meant to be offensive. But that's just the way it is, if someone starts to complain after eight and a half hours of work, then they should do an internship or work as a nurse or doctor in the healthcare sector, and that even in difficult Corona times. Use this example as a source of energy to make it clear to yourself that you are tired, but studying for 2 hours in the evening is not a knockout.

There are always people who always work more and do more, but one must also realize that one must not become soft inside. And if you go to an event for two hours in the evening after a ten-hour day on Tuesday, don't feel sorry for yourself and complain. You should pull yourself together, look in the mirror and ask yourself where you want to go.

If you don't want to achieve anything, then stay at home, lie in front of the TV and watch some third-rate satire or some sports event, and if you want to network, meet people, hear new things, also outside of your actual professional field, then use the opportunities, accept invitations, ask friends or professional contacts if there is something, and the internet offers you so many information possibilities.

Try to actively get involved in networking, get to know the people, exchange your contact details and simply see it as a long-term time investment. Contacts grow over many years and many contacts you won't even have to ask if they will answer your questions or support you in a project. You never know beforehand which of the 500 or 5000 contacts can support you, answer your questions or simply give you information on the short service route in five or ten years.

You should also see this as a personality-building measure, expand your horizon, and also get rid of the idea that you are practically only making contacts in order to benefit from them later. Because you should also see the other perspective, the other people who go to an event to also meet new people, hear new views, perspectives and experiences, they also depend on you, on people who then go to such an event. This is a win-win situation for all involved. This of course requires a high time commitment, dedication and sharp time discipline, a prioritization, what do I spend my time on. You also have to burden yourself a bit, if it is a bit exhausting on the day, then you simply have to go directly under the shower when you come from the event and jump into bed immediately, instead of watching some series until 02:00 in the morning. Then you are reasonably fit the next day. It depends on your decisions and your personal discipline.

And networking is an essential component for long-term success, to achieve goals efficiently.

Franzen and Hangartner (2005) conclude in their article on "Social Networks and Professional Success" about the hypothesis of Granovetter (1973, 1974, 1995) that mediation through personal networks is advantageous for placement in the job market. The summary of their scientific article states:

> "While this thesis has long been considered undisputed in sociology, newer empirical studies surprisingly seem to refute it. However, most studies limit themselves to analyzing the monetary consequences of job finding through social contacts. We also focus on the analysis of non-monetary job characteristics, such as the adequacy of education. The data basis is the information from 8000 Swiss university graduates who started their professional career between the end of 2000 and the beginning of 2001, one year after graduation. The results show that the search for a job through personal relationships is widespread. On the one hand, our analyses also show that graduates who found a job through personal networks cannot achieve an income advantage. On the other hand, the results suggest that placement through social networks is associated with a higher adequacy of education. In addition, jobs found through social contacts are more often referred to as career investments, in which the graduates can better apply their skills than in jobs reached through formal search strategies. Additionally, the search through social contacts is associated with lower search costs. Overall, the non-monetary aspects of jobs seem to be particularly advantageous when mediated through personal networks."

Franzen and Hangartner (2005) refer to Granovetter (1973, 1974, 1995), who also demonstrated in further studies (2005) that social structures, networks, and shared values can influence economic outcomes. Recently, Granovetter (2018) has been dealing with sociology in economic life and introduces in his book up to the 18th century to report on the history of "Economic Sociology".

These insights into the scientific evaluation of network activities, whether for individuals, interest groups, companies or groups of companies, should show you that it can result in a conscious or unconscious decision on your part to decide to work harder on your network engagements in the long term. It involves time commitment, dedication, and effort, but just like in a football game with extra time and penalty shootouts, it doesn't work without a 100% full throttle mentality and the same conditions apply to all other competitors on your way to the pole star. You can now become aware that it is entirely up to you whether you build a strong network or not, no one is stopping you. Go for it, good luck!

References

Böttger, M., Weilandt, M., & Braun, O. L. (2019). Zeitmanagement. In *Selbstmanagement und mentale Stärke im Arbeitsleben* (pp. 21–36). Springer.

Covey, S. R., Merrill, A. R., Merrill, R. R., & Altmann, A. (2014). *Der Weg zum Wesentlichen: der Klassiker des Zeitmanagements*. Campus.

Däfler, M. N. (2018). Zeitmanagement-Methoden anwenden. In *Gib mir Geduld – aber flott!* (pp. 241–259). Springer.

Franzen, A., & Hangartner, D. (2005). Soziale Netzwerke und beruflicher Erfolg. *KZfSS Kölner Zeitschrift für Soziologie und Sozialpsychologie, 57*(3), 443–465.

Goodman, R., Scott, S., & Rothenberger, A. (2000). Hyperaktivität. In *Kinderpsychiatrie kompakt* (pp. 77–87). Steinkopff/Springer.

Granovetter, M. (1974). Granovetter replies to Gans. *American Journal of Sociology, 80*(2), 527–529. University of Chicago Press.

Granovetter, M. (1995). Coase revisited: Business groups in the modern economy. *Industrial and Corporate Change, 4*(1), 93–130.

Granovetter, M. (2005). The impact of social structure on economic outcomes. *Journal of Economic Perspectives, 19*(1), 33–50.

Granovetter, M. (2018). *The sociology of economic life*. Routledge.

Granovetter, M. S. (1973). The strength of weak ties. *American Journal of Sociology, 78*(6), 1360–1380.

Quernheim, G. (2018). Zeitmanagement. In *Und jetzt Sie! – Selbst-und Zeitmanagement in Gesundheitsberufen* (pp. 127–150). Springer.

Rusch, S. (2019). Zeitmanagement. In *Stressmanagement* (pp. 113–123). Springer.

Seiwert, L. (2012). *30 Minuten Zeitmanagement*. GABAL Verlag GmbH.

4

Accept Competition and go Full Throttle

We are in constant competition, both privately and professionally. The sooner you accept this, the better. Of course, there are different phases of intensity in life, and competition is not always immediately visible.

Whether it's a good job, a good starting position for your own business, contracts, life partners, a spot by the pool on vacation, or medals in sports—there's always someone else who wants the same thing. Does that surprise you?

There are different ways to deal with this situation, either by complaining and wishing for a planet where no competition exists, or by accepting it positively and working hard and constantly to improve your ranking. Your choice!

The starting point in the competition of life can vary, in disadvantaged residential areas (Friedrichs and Blasius 2000), in poverty (Meier et al. 2013), depending on the income strength of the household (Schupp et al. 2003), personal cognitive abilities (Schmidt-Atzert et al. 2004), access to early childhood education (Schlotter and Wößmann 2010), coming from a non-academic or academic household (Peter and Wittenberg 2016; Wienert 2006), conditions in school (Eichhorn 2008), the tendency towards perfectionism (Spitzer 2016) or exaggerated expectations of parents up to systemic family therapy (Nemetschek 2013). Everyone has, as they say, their own burden to bear, and it's up to us how we deal with the starting point. Please always remember:

> **Tip**
> The winner is not recognized at the start, but at the finish line!

4.1 Sports Experiences and Professional Competition

After presenting at the Open and User Innovation Conference (OUI) at Harvard Business School (Boston, USA) in 2014 and 2016, and having an exchange of experiences on teaching methods at the Harvard Innovation Lab and the MIT Media Lab in March 2015, I also used my experiences from the Second World of Innovation Conference (WOIC) in Silicon Valley (USA) in November 2015, which was organized by the University of California, Berkeley, and incorporated various things with regard to sports experiences and professional competition. I also presented a study at the Singapore Economic Review Conference (SERC) in 2017. The question was whether some company founders build up a certain resilience due to experiences from school and club sports in their youth,

4 Accept Competition and go Full Throttle

for example in the medical device and medical technology industry, and to what extent the relevance of these sports experiences has an influence on leadership competence. Professor Dr. Sabrina Krauss will give a detailed overview on the topic of resilience itself in subchapter 4.5.

Now to the study: I had already published on this topic, how sports experiences influence company founders, in the journal Ideas and Innovation Management, published by the German Institute for Business Administration (43rd volume/03.17), in 2017. The following was the focus:

In the study design, we chose an empirical approach at the time and wanted to check whether sports experiences at competition level during youth, regardless of whether it is individual or team sports, through experiences such as training, performance improvement through training, injuries, goal setting, team or individual performance, player/coach relationships and victories/defeats, whether this leads to a further development of the persons, whether they build up mental strength through this and whether this has an influence on the company founders and the development of the companies. Between January 2015 and January 2017, we surveyed 48 company founders from the medical device and medical technology industry in two stages, who were then in the Netherlands, Belgium and Germany. Five questions were asked. In the first stage (survey of all 48 company founders):

1. Did you participate in a sport for at least five years during your school time, either at school or in a club, and regularly attend training?
2. Was it a team sport or an individual sport?
3. In addition to training, did you regularly participate in competitions in the club or in city championships?

Furthermore, we also asked whether these sports experiences from youth had an influence on later business activities. And in this case, we surveyed companies that were younger than ten years. It was important that the founders were still active in the management. Of the 48 surveyed company founders and executives, 34 people were those who had regularly trained sports for at least five years in their youth and participated in competitions. And of these 34, who had experienced competitive sports in their youth, 85.3 percent stated that this had helped them in the later founding of the company. And 67.65 percent stated that without these experiences from their current assessment, without this sports experience from their youth, they would not have been able to build the company as successfully.

At that time, we came to the application-oriented conclusion that it is understandable that sports training and competition experiences in youth are personality-forming and promote perseverance, resilience, and competitive fighting behavior. And we saw this confirmed in the responses of the company founders and executives. We interpreted this to the extent that as a company founder, from the sports experience in youth, one knows that there are highs and lows, victories and defeats, and that above-average hard work and effort in competition lead to lasting success. The study confirmed, within the manageable pool of respondents, that the influence of sports experience from youth on company founders of innovative small and medium-sized companies in the medical device and medical technology industry, with particular consideration of the complex of resilience, could contribute to perseverance, and that great importance should also be placed on physical fitness and interaction in a sports context in schools and social work, also with regard to training and competition. The positive influence on personality development could also be underlined. We then agreed that we would recommend follow-up studies.

At this point, I may share with you the interim results of the follow-up study on these study results from the years 2016/2017: Between February and May 2019, we surveyed (of the total 31 respondents, 24 were men and seven women) twice on site, twice in London (UK) once 16 and once 15 company founders (inclusion criteria: age of respondents 20–40 years), whose start-up companies were exclusively active in the technology sector and the companies were not older than three years, about their experiences. Important as preliminary results (the final statistical evaluations have not yet been made): All respondents stated that they had experienced sports and competition in their youth and college or university time, interestingly, of the 31 respondents, 26 were active in individual sports, namely horse riding, golf, tennis or boxing. While my initial assessments in the study from the years 2016/2017 were that team sports were the decisive factor here, it seems to be the case that the athletic competition with other individuals, and horse riding, golf, tennis and boxing are sports where you have to compete alone, similar to athletics in many disciplines, that the competitive pressure, the competition experience and the survival in this situation, so not the team sport, but **the direct athletic competition itself, could be the decisive factor**, but of course further studies are to be pursued here.

Figure 4.1 clearly shows that the will to succeed must never wane. Whether victory or defeat, the will to succeed, the hunger to develop further, remains:

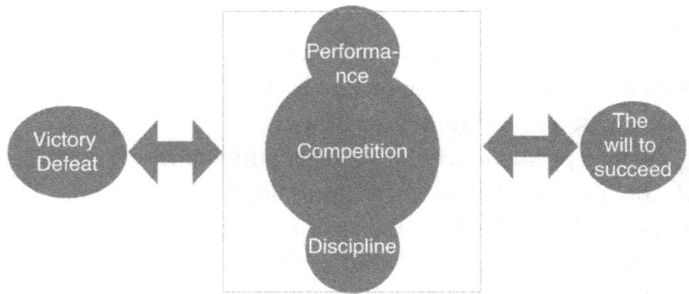

Fig. 4.1 "Permanent competition mode" according to Plugmann (own illustration). This figure describes that the will to succeed never wanes

4.2 Guest Commentary Assina Müller "(Team) Sports in Youth Toughens Up" (Former Handball Bundesliga Player, Master's Student and Physiotherapist, B. Sc.)

The saying "Sport toughens you up" is widely spread among the general public. Countless studies prove that regular physical training prevents many risks. However, the right dosage is crucial. Physical training can be dosed like a medication: ineffective, optimal, but also to the point where it becomes a poison. Especially in early childhood, sport has a tremendous influence on the physical and psychological development of the child (Janssen and LeBlanc 2010). Nevertheless, according to the 4th Children and Youth Sports Report (2020), about 80 percent of children and adolescents in Germany are not active enough (Breuer et al. 2020). They all fall short of the World Health Organization's recommended daily physical activity (at least 60 minutes a day, primarily of moderate to high-intensity aerobic activity; World Health Organization 2018). A look into kindergartens, schools, and sports clubs confirms this picture. Sport has always played a significant role in the lives of young people. However, the conditions have changed. The daily life of many children and adolescents is characterized by early and all-day visits to daycare centers and kindergartens, a changed structure of the school system, the emergence of new leisure activities, and digital networking through smartphones and social networks. Increased sedentary activity, lack of physical exercise, and increased poor nutrition result in overweight/obesity and chronic, sometimes nutrition-dependent diseases already in early childhood. In addition to individual health consequences, social societal consequences are also increasingly coming into focus at an early age (Oberger et al. 2010).

The fine line of the right dosage of athletic training has occupied me for many years. As a former handball Bundesliga player and coach in the performance and junior sector, I was able to make my own experiences with these challenges every day. When I had my first encounter with handball at the age of four, I didn't know where my athletic path would lead me. In my first training session, my brother threw a handball at my head. Out of defiance, I said to him, "Wait, my dear, you'll get that back someday." My brother was bigger, stronger, and quicker. Nevertheless, I had a goal and a strong intrinsic motivation, I wanted to be better than him. Looking back, I can say that I achieved this athletically. But how did I manage to get from a modest village club, through district and state selections to the national top? And did sport toughen me up for my later life?

Sport has many positive effects that relate to the physical and psychological aspects of the body. But what exactly is it that toughens up children and adolescents through sport?

From my personal experience, I can report a formative event. After I had discovered handball playing for myself after some time, I made a decisive decision. I announced that I would play in the women's handball Bundesliga one day. My family, friends, teammates, and coaches laughed at me for my project. I was not the most talented player, but I had the right attitude, ambition, and will to achieve my goal. My goal was clearly defined, it was SMART—specific, measurable, attractive, realistic, and timed. My ambition was aroused to show my environment that will and my motivation can move mountains and I will achieve my goal.

I believe that the right combination of various individual skills and abilities shapes children and adolescents for their later life through sport. Children have a natural urge to move. They actively get to know their environment, they develop through movement. And not only in the area of motor skills, but also emotionally, (psycho)socially, and cognitively. In addition to social interaction, children learn early on to duel in a playful way. Competition has a different meaning than in later professional life. Children learn to deal with defeats and to celebrate successes together. The team idea is conveyed to children early on. They should learn to integrate even the seemingly weakest link into the group and achieve team success together. Already Alexandre Dumas the Elder proclaimed in 1844 in his historical novel "Les Trois Mousquetaires" the core idea of team sports: "Unus pro omnibus, omnes pro uno—One for all and all for one!" (Dumas the Elder 1844).

Sport is, despite the changed societal conditions, still the number 1 extracurricular leisure activity for children and adolescents. Especially in childhood and adolescence, sport is practiced in clubs. This can be associated with social recognition as well as a strengthening of self-esteem and self-efficacy. This results in so-called "social skills," which are considered a basic requirement in today's working world. Children are shaped by sport and learn in a playful way to take a place in today's increasingly demanding, performance-oriented, and fast-paced world.

In conclusion, it should be noted that success begins in the mind—whether in professional life, private life, or sport. Sport offers the opportunity already in early childhood to be successful on various levels. Albert Schweitzer once said: "Success is not the key to happiness, but happiness is the key to success. If you love what you are doing, you will be successful." Children should be allowed to get to know their athletic abilities and skills in an unforced and naive way. Because only then can they experience sport in its entirety and benefit from it throughout their lives.

4.3 Principle of Highest Urgency

Have you ever seen a center forward in football leisurely storming the opposing goal, or a basketball player casually heading to the opposing basket during a fastbreak? Of course not, that's illogical.

Why is it in sports quite normal to act according to the principle of highest urgency if you want to succeed, but in professional or private life some people seem to have taken a sleeping pill and move towards the goal at a speed as if they had 100 years? It can be made clear that for certain opportunities or chances only a limited time window is open. If you do not go through this time window within a certain time and thus let the opportunity pass by, it may well be that it takes a long time until this opportunity arises again and a time window opens again.

> **Tip**
>
> Tip: Always act according to the principle of highest urgency!

This means that you want things to be done quickly. It's always nice when you are the factor and you can influence the control when it comes to completing a certain work package in a timely manner, seizing an opportunity or driving things forward. It becomes more difficult when the use of this opportunity depends on third parties. Then you can put pressure. Putting pressure means there will be conflicts. You call people, you ask if they are finished, when the documents are coming, or why this or that project section has not yet been handed over as agreed. Pressure builds up. If things go well, everything will be done in your favor. Otherwise, there will be conflicts. This means that on the way to success you will also have to take conflict training or practice it, because unfortunately it often only works by putting pressure on others. In doing so, you don't just make friends. Therefore, you must always give the other person the opportunity to improve the situation and never push it to the extreme that the other person loses face. Even under pressure, FAIR PLAY applies, which is a good basis for long-term and trustworthy cooperation.

Make Decisions Quickly

In order to be able to act quickly and implement the principle of highest urgency, you need to make decisions quickly. This means that you need to establish certain criteria for how to make decisions in a short period of time. For example, an apartment is for sale at a good price—buy or not buy. You want to complete a further education course while working. The course starts in six weeks.

4 Accept Competition and go Full Throttle

You have three universities to choose from. You have to choose one, because you have to consider that there is still registration time, that you need an acceptance, and that you may have to discuss this with your employer or your company.

Holiday trip is offered at a good price, but you only have three days to book—book or not book. You are asked if you can volunteer in a certain organization once a month, or if you can participate in a donation campaign that runs for another two days—yes or no. According to which criteria can you make decisions quickly: First of all, you have to abandon the idea that you can always make the right decision, because you make the decision at a time T0 and evaluate this decision-making process in the time window T1, i.e. weeks, months or years later. The conditions are different, the insights have also grown and thus the situation and basis on which you made this decision are different.

So you will always make a percentage of wrong decisions. This cannot be prevented. But if you generally wait until the opportunities are no longer given, then you will probably not be able to seize many opportunities (and make few mistakes). Conversely, this means that you have to take risks when making decisions in order to be successful. And if you are risk-affine, i.e. you like to take risks and are also willing to bear the consequences, i.e. financial, time or reputation loss, then you will make decisions more often, and also more often risk-affine decisions. If you are more of a safety player and prefer not to take any risks at all, then you will not make decisions until the opportunities that open up in front of you are no longer given, or you will often reject offers. This is the spectrum and the problem with decisions. Basically, if you are interested in an opportunity, if an opportunity presents itself and you decide to participate or take part, then you must decide according to the principle of highest urgency, because the competition does not sleep and the time window does not stay open forever.

4.4 Expertise Wins: Knowledge of Products and Services

No matter what industry you work in, you deal directly or indirectly with products and services. This means that you need to be well acquainted with the products and services. The areas in which you operate, whether it's B2B, business to business, or B2C, business to customer, come with different requirements, but ultimately you need to have answers to the customers' question of why they should buy from you, or why they should use your services. This means that you prepare for the conversations with a list of objections. As is known from various industries, the typical customer responses "no time", "no interest", "no money" are the same as there are certain objection strategies in sales to respond to them. However, you must conversely know your products and services excellently. This includes expertise and also the perspective of what the customers who want to use your products or services have in it. To put it bluntly: If you are asked "Why should I use your product" or "Your service? What is the unique selling point?", then you must be well prepared to answer these questions—in depth and in breadth. You must be an expert and accordingly, when you are in direct conversation, you must present yourself linguistically, physically, and vocally.

Authenticity plays an important role in this, among many other aspects. For example, I personally attended

4 Accept Competition and go Full Throttle

a multi-day training course 15 years ago where I gave a short presentation. The group of course participants consisted of twelve people. Everyone could give a few minutes presentation on a topic of their choice and was filmed with a video camera. That was the first time I saw myself speaking on a video camera. And interestingly, I always liked to take an "intellectual pause" during the presentations because I thought it gave the presentation a certain intellectual touch. But when I saw myself speaking on the video, I was worried that I was having a heart attack because the pause was so infinitely long for the viewer that they thought "Has he forgotten his text or is he doing a system relaunch?". I would highly recommend that you do some speaking exercises, get recorded. Nowadays, this is of course a very simple thing with a smartphone. Just arrange with friends who also occasionally give presentations or are regularly in contact with customers and then rate each other. This can certainly have a playful component and is a great leisure activity for a Saturday evening.

You realize that you can always improve. The way you stand, your posture, the way you speak, how you modulate your voice, and how your arguments are, lead to you reflecting and improving. So there is no second chance for the appearance and also for the first impression. You can only present yourself for the first time once. It is important, if you want to be successful, that you have excellent knowledge ("Top-10%") about the products and services you offer and are simply an expert and stand firm. And sometimes you have to make decisions. Do I now spend 2000 euros for a multi-day communication training and improve my appearance, my communication, and my argumentation or do I go on vacation for the third or fourth time this year.

If money should be tight, then you have to make a decision. And here, foregoing vacation is certainly an alternative or the sports rims for the car. You just have to set priorities. And the highest priority to achieve the set goals is that you personally also make some sacrifices. It may be that in extreme cases you even sell your car and travel around by tram for half a year or a year. If that's the sacrifice you have to make to achieve your goal, then that's the way it is. But it will be worth it—it comes back tenfold. The increase in expertise is of course not only that you know your own products and services well, but also those of the most important competitors. This is an extra effort that you have to make, because you are always in competition, both in terms of technical specifications, for example if it is medical technology products, in terms of pricing, financing and also service agreements, as well as telephone accessibility and other secondary factors. So it is important that you also know the competitor's products and their services. This extra effort is worth it, because then you can have a deeper conversation with potentially new customers or existing customers who want to leave, highlight quality and guarantee features, and create an individual offer that represents a compromise, but still wins the customer for your own company.

You can see your homework in Fig. 4.2, please check in which area you could improve. Expertise, professional preparation, and a very good first impression are the basis for successful long-term relationships with other people. Many companies today differentiate themselves more through relationship management with the customer. Combined with excellent expertise, you have the best possible chances of success:

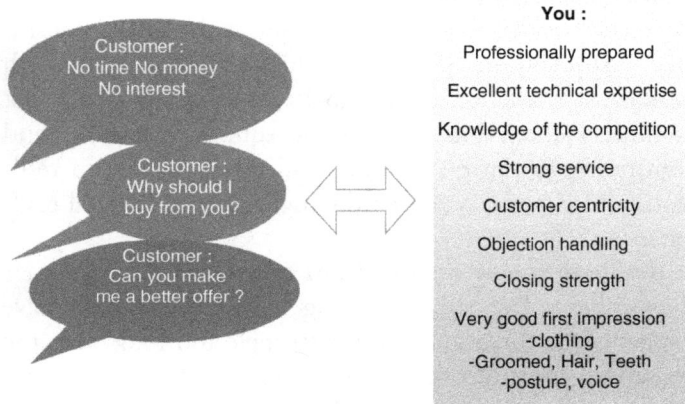

Fig. 4.2 "Expertise means professional preparation" according to Plugmann (own illustration). This figure describes your homework that you should do to achieve your goals

4.5 Guest Contribution RESILIENCE by Prof. Dr. Sabrina Krauss, SRH University in North Rhine-Westphalia

4.5.1 Resilience

The term resilience describes the psychological resilience of a person (Brinkmann 2014); that is, the ability to overcome crises and to become satisfied and happy again even after severe setbacks. In recent studies, the term is further expanded and, for example, extended to companies or even leadership behavior (Pauls et al. 2019). In this chapter, the focus should be on individual resilience. The benefits of resilience for the individual and the possibility of further enhancing existing resilience should be considered. Especially in relation to achieving goals, it is worth looking at resilience, as few goals are achieved at the first attempt. Failing, enduring the subsequent frustration, and continuing to pursue the goal—all this is related to resilience and is better achieved the higher the individual resilience is.

Resilient people recover from crises and failures faster than others. They find meaning in the events that have happened to them and do not struggle too long with the perceived injustices that come with them. Interesting research on resilience emerged, for example, when Emmy Werner found in a large-scale longitudinal study on the island of Kaui (Hawaii) that children who grew up under adverse circumstances (poverty, violence, heavy alcohol consumption by parents, etc.) did not necessarily develop a mental illness (Werner 2011) or even follow the same destructive life path as their parents. There were children who repeated the sad fate, but there were also many children who managed to lead a satisfied life despite all difficulties and leave the crisis-ridden childhood behind. The children who managed to lead a satisfied life were referred to as resilient. This example shows that almost all of us can overcome a crisis, even emerge stronger from it. This also means that our past cannot necessarily be used as an excuse for today's standstill or discontent. People are not at the mercy of their past. We can all start anew, set new goals, and create new things. This does not mean that this path will be easy, or that it would be easy, but it means that we can make it. However, only if we really want to, because performance always also consists of the "wanting". One could say: performance is "can times want". Or: "Who does not want, cannot!"

Sometimes it is discussed whether the construct "resilience" is a personality trait or a trainable ability. Experience and some research approaches, e.g. the *Comprehensive Soldier Fitness Program* of the US Army (Harms et al. 2013), show that training one's own resilience can certainly be worthwhile, which will be described in more detail below.

Of course, not every failure is a crisis, but it is not always easy to deal with a failure and to invest the remaining energy less in complaining or condemning the current situation, but to use it to tackle a goal again. But this is exactly where one of the key factors of resilient people lies, those who recover faster. Crises, failures, and difficult situations are inseparable from human existence. So when a challenging situation arises, one can react in different ways: one could mourn the circumstance or be angry that it has come to this. But neither anger nor grief will change the past. So one could also accept what has happened and refocus on what one wants to achieve. Dealing with a situation always also involves a decision. It is usually not the situations that drain our energy for so long, but rather our evaluations of the situation. Certainly, the implementation is not quite easy, but it starts with a decision. The decision not to hold on to suffering or pain longer than necessary. The more often we make this decision, the more we can internalize this approach and train our resilience.

It is also helpful to build a social network that strengthens and nourishes us. Resilient people often have stable relationships and bonds with other people who listen to them in difficult times and give them strength. Social relationships are not only helpful in times of crisis, but the beautiful moments can also be perceived as even more beautiful through a shared experience. A good exercise for reflecting on one's own social contacts is to "draw" the people one contacts more frequently. These people can be represented on a piece of paper as circles, for example, with the names of the respective person written in the circle. One represents oneself on the same piece of paper as a cross in the middle. Now mark all people with whom the contact is not exclusively positive, with a red line between the cross and the respective circle. The people who are helpful, supportive, and very pleasant to contact are marked with a green line. In the sense of strengthening resilience, one can thus intensify contact with the people with the green lines and minimize or change the relationship with the people with the red lines, so that the line may change its color from red to green.

It can also be effective to write down ten things you enjoy doing to strengthen your personal resources. These things should then be carried out or implemented in daily life as often as possible. This simple exercise also encourages reflection on how you manage your own time. To further strengthen your own resilience, it can also be effective to briefly note down the positive events of the day each evening, thus directing your own focus towards the positive and strengthening aspects, from which new strength can be drawn. These can of course also be small things, like a pleasant encounter or a compliment. Most people only remember what went wrong during the day. However, this type of memory only robs further energies.

So, there are many ways to strengthen your own resilience and influence your own life.

In summary, this means:

- Make the decision to accept already occurred annoyances (crises) and not to waste any more energy on them.
- Reflect on and maintain your social network.

- Write down ten things you enjoy doing and then implement them.
- Focus on the positive things in everyday life.

Being or becoming resilient does not mean no longer experiencing crises, resilient behavior can rather be compared to a blade of grass that can be pressed down by a strong wind, but as soon as the wind is over, it stands up strong and upright again. In addition, we should all realize that failure, crises, and disappointments are part of life and are usually far less severe than we often judge them to be. Constructive handling of failures can be practiced, certainly not by setting no new or only very simple goals. See failure as an opportunity; an opportunity to learn and to deploy and train your own resilience. Dare to do something. Set goals and pursue them. Motivated, confident, and resilient.

References

Breuer, C., Joisten, C., & Schmidt, W. (Eds.). (2020). *Vierter Kinder- und Jugendsportbericht – Gesundheit, Leistung, Gesellschaft*. Hofmann.

Brinkmann, R. (2014). *Angewandte Gesundheitspsychologie* (p. 137). Pearson.

Dumas der Ältere, A. (1844). *Les Trois Mousquetaires*. Übersetzt von Bräuning, H. (2011). Anaconda.

Eichhorn, C. (2008). *Classroom-Management: Wie Lehrer, Eltern und Schüler guten Unterricht gestalten*. Klett-Cotta.

Friedrichs, J., & Blasius, J. (2000). *Leben in benachteiligten Wohngebieten*. Leske und Budrich.

Harms, P. D., Herian, M., Krasikova, D. V., Vanhove, A. J., & Lester, P. B. (2013). *The comprehensive soldier and family fitness program evaluation. Report #4: Evaluation of resilience training and mental and behavioral health outcomes* (p. 10). P. D. Harms Publications.

Janssen, I., & LeBlanc, A. (2010). Systematische Überprüfung der gesundheitlichen Vorteile von körperlicher Aktivität und Fitness bei Kindern und Jugendlichen im schulischen Alter. *International Journal of Behavioral Nutrition and Physical Activity, 7*(40), 1–16.

Meier, U., Preuße, H., & Sunnus, E. M. (2013). *Steckbriefe von Armut: Haushalte in prekären Lebenslagen.* Springer.

Nemetschek, P. (2013). *Systemische Familientherapie mit Kinder, Jugendlichen und Eltern: Lebensfluss-Modelle und analoge Methoden.* Klett-Cotta.

Oberger, J., Opper, E., Karger, C., Worth, A., Geuder, J., & Bös, K. (2010). Motorische Leistungsfähigkeit als Indikator für die Gesundheit von Kindern und Jugendlichen. *Monatsschrift Kinderheilkunde, 158*(5), 441–448.

Pauls, N., Schlett, C., & Soucek, R. (2019). Organisationale Resilienz. *Zeitschrift für Arbeits- und Organisationspsychologie, 63,* 110–112. https://doi.org/10.1026/0932-4089/a000296.

Peter, F., & Wittenberg, E. (2016). Kinder aus Nichtakademiker-Haushalten wollen nach einem Infoworkshop eher studieren: Sieben Fragen an Frauke Peter. *DIW Wochenbericht, 83*(26), 566–566.

Schlotter, M., & Wößmann, L. (2010). Frühkindliche Bildung und spätere kognitive und nichtkognitive Fähigkeiten: Deutsche und internationale Evidenz. *Vierteljahrshefte zur Wirtschaftsforschung, 79*(3), 99–120.

Schmidt-Atzert, L., Deter, B., & Jaeckel, S. (2004). Prädiktion von Ausbildungserfolg: Allgemeine Intelligenz (g) oder spezifische kognitive Fähigkeiten? *Zeitschrift für Personalpsychologie, 3*(4), 147–158.

Schupp, J., Gramlich, T., Isengard, B., Pischner, R., Wagner, G. G., & Rosenblatt, B. V. (2003). Repräsentative Analyse der Lebenslagen einkommensstarker Haushalte. Studie des DIW Berlin im Auftrag des Bundesministeriums für Gesundheit und Soziale Sicherung.

Spitzer, N. (2016). Perfektionismus und klinischer Perfektionismus – Definitionen und mögliche Ursachen. In *Perfektionismus und seine vielfältigen psychischen Folgen* (pp. 25–37). Springer.

Werner, E. (2011). Risiko und Resilienz im Leben von Kindern aus multiethnischen Familien. In M. Zander (Ed.), *Handbuch Resilienzförderung* (pp. 32–46). VS Verlag.

Wienert, H. (2006). Einkommensdifferenzen zwischen Nicht-Akademikern und Akademikern. *Wirtschaftsdienst, 86*(2), 105–111.

World Health Organization. (2018). *Global action plan on physical activity 2018–2030: More active people for a healthier world.* https://apps.who.int/iris/bitstream/handle/10665/272722/9789241514187-eng.pdf?sequence=1&isAllowed=y. Accessed: 2. Mai 2021.

5

The Decision for the Personal Innovation Process

The transformation of the mindset corresponds to a personal reprogramming. The hardest part is to make a decision now, after you have read in the previous chapters what sacrifices and what persistent relentless effort are required. In this process, similar to the innovation processes in the development of innovative products and services, you can use these to generate ideas and move into concrete implementation, in the design and transformation of your new mindset. It is also important to accept reality, not to sugarcoat your own situation and to unlearn wishful thinking. You become an unyielding uncompromising learning and working machine, and that in the best sense. Please rate this expression positively. Striving obsessively or obsessively for goals and victories should have a positive image and not be pressed into negative disease patterns. Everyone has the right to voluntarily achieve more and want to make more out of their life. Personal will is and remains a private matter.

As so often, one tends to give a lot of space in one's own thought world to things that were hard to stomach in the past, be it defeats, unpleasant encounters with other people, or simply negative emotions associated with memories of certain situations.

You may say goodbye to this with immediate effect, and I would like to give you the following "95/5 rule" as a recommendation for action:

5.1 The 95/5 Rule

To stay motivated and efficient in the long term, one should have and maintain a positive basic attitude. This also includes not losing perspective on the things that one has successfully created and accomplished. Sometimes people tend to focus on what didn't work, a kind of heroic attempt at perfectionism with the goal or approach of doing everything right. This is, of course, an energy-draining attitude. Of course, if you have a company or if you do a certain self-analysis, you also have to think about the things that did not go optimally and draw conclusions from them. But overall, on the way to the next intermediate goal, one should be aware that one has already completed numerous work packages and should also write these positively into the duty book.

So, for example, if you have been very diligent in the last four weeks, have regularly got up early, have carried out your learning and work goals, your presentation, exercises, whatever had to be done, then you have achieved a lot during this time, you can be proud of this and must also visualize these achievements and performance packages, to which you can tick off, positively. This lifts the mood, makes it clear once again that you have been diligent and productive in the past weeks, and if there were a few things that did not work so well, even if it was a brutal failure, do not lose your sense of humor, yes, humor is when you laugh anyway, and try to identify the causes with a factual reflection so that you can do better next time or this mistake does not repeat itself as much as possible.

Sometimes the reasons are that there was not enough time, that the planning was too ambitious, and so one can draw conclusions from small, medium, and large defeats. Nevertheless, think of the many things that you have done very well, your commitment, your attitude, and also praise yourself so that you always maintain the positive basic attitude. This is the foundation from which you draw the strength to make further plans and then implement them. The nice thing about the 95/5 rule is, I personally do not know anyone who could permanently bring about a 100/0 situation. There is always a little loss, whether you are entrepreneurial, employed, learning, or in a private environment. The so-called "perfect" should of course be visualized somewhere in the back of your mind, but you must not make a drama out of it if you have a 5% deviation in the area of your goal setting and implementation. 95% is already a very good value, and it took me a very, very long time to get to this area in my personal goal planning and implementation at all. There were also times when it was "fifty-fifty" or "seventy-five-twenty-five" and it takes a certain time until you settle in there. Always keep your focus on the positive.

5.2 Discipline and Continuity

Many myths revolve around the word discipline, and you get different definitions from all possible directions. For example, I remember a video from the internet where a high-ranking general tells his listeners: "Yes, you have to make your bed perfectly every morning after you get up. And if you are not able to leave your bed almost perfectly, if you fail at that, how do you want to achieve something in life or change the world?"

I have never left the bed properly in my life and yet it worked well with the job and privately. And yes, even my father tried to teach me discipline in my youth by pulling the blanket off me at seven o'clock on Sunday mornings, opening the window and saying: "So, get up and do something".

In my perception, these activities have no direct causal connection to a success plan, because without an individual time flow diagram and the corresponding implementation strategy, embedded in an overall concept, where you become a permanent learning and working machine and improve from year to year, these small impulses bring nothing. It even suggests the wrong impression, as if the success concept was so simple, if you go to bed early or make your bed perfectly after you get up or get up very early on Sundays, as if everything was solved with this single impulse. Of course, this is not the case. Discipline often reflects on various levels:

Discipline Your Thoughts

Discipline also means gaining control over what you think, how you think, and how you value and assess yourself. You are probably familiar with this. **Positive thinking** is not just a flippant expression, but you have to put yourself in a positive basic mood in which you firmly believe that you will achieve the set goals, and also have confidence in yourself that you will implement and apply everything necessary to successfully achieve these goals and the cascade of planning and implementing one goal after another. You are responsible for your state of mind

5 The Decision for the Personal Innovation Process

and only you can change this state. If you are in a high phase, feeling fit, positively motivated, perhaps in a phase shortly after a success experience, then you could run jubilantly through the streets and shout out your happiness. And if the last success is longer ago and you find yourself in a difficult situation, there is always the risk of becoming a bit depressive or negative thinking, and this of course also manifests itself in your physical and mental condition. You have to counteract this, which means you have to be disciplined when you notice that you start to doubt or let concerns from your environment get to you and no longer bounce off.

Then it's time to discipline yourself back towards positive thinking and visualize that you will achieve the goal, and have confidence in yourself. This is of course exhausting, but unavoidable. Not only physical work or fitness training are exhausting, but also control over the overall mental state, constantly inspiring yourself positively, motivating yourself and controlling your thoughts in a disciplined way.

It makes a difference whether you are positive-optimistic and full of drive or whether you have already given up on yourself and no longer believe in achieving your goal. **You must never give up.** And this mental discipline is sometimes more exhausting than physical work. In phases where you don't feel mentally fit and feel less motivated, I recommend the so-called "salami tactic". This really means taking one step at a time and not thinking: Will I achieve the goal or not? Are the probabilities high that I will achieve it or not? But to focus on the daily business, that is, I have my time flow diagram, I know what work and learning performance I have to achieve on this day or this week, and I focus on implementing the implementation plan in the next one, two, three days. And just as a squirrel takes on nut after nut, we work our way step by step, from day to day, from week to week. And if we pull it through, then the probability is high that success will be at the end of this chain of actions.

It is often heard that especially high-performance athletes talk about it, but also very successful people in their profession, that they visualize their success, that they use various visualization techniques. They imagine a certain movement sequence or a certain event. Whatever the technique may be, in the end it is about putting yourself in a positive basic mood, which is characterized by optimism, confidence, self-confidence and appreciation. My personal conviction is that with the multitude of techniques and methods offered, everyone knows best for themselves what the right trigger is. Because no one knows you as well as you know yourself. I would simply recommend listening to yourself, constantly reminding yourself that you are a positive person with a goal, that you have written down this goal on the goal flow diagram, what you have to achieve for it, what you have to sacrifice for it, and to pull it through in the implementation phase.

Then the positive basic mood comes all by itself, because you see day by day that you are implementing. This also increases self-confidence and leads to the achievement of the goal in the end. Some people get up in the morning and look in the mirror, motivate themselves for a few minutes, others eat something specific and others go for a run in the morning, do sports exercises or do something else. Over time, you simply develop a system to keep yourself in a predominantly positive mood from the beginning of the day to bedtime. And for this you also simply have to take the bird's eye view and be aware that you are on the way to the next goal, which is also very nice. Enjoy your very personal adventure journey!

The discipline of constantly being in a positive mindset can of course be very exhausting. You can be very proud of yourself. Realize what you have achieved so far, what you are achieving and what you will achieve, what this means for you, for your family and what opportunities lie ahead of you. And you can assume that the human brain can learn everything and that you as a person can achieve performances and that there are hardly any limitations. Of course, there are limitations, not everyone will be a Nobel laureate and not everyone can found a company like Facebook or Google. But there are hundreds of thousands of professional careers and private happiness, so you don't have to be among the Olympic winners to lead a professionally and privately happy life. Instead, you simply have to work towards your set goal day by day through goal orientation, discipline, diligence, resilience, optimism, drive and reliability, and you will then achieve it.

This is fantastic news. So, you don't have to win the Champions League final in sports or become a Bundesliga champion, nor do you have to run 100 meters in under ten seconds or throw spears and balls, but you can simply join the group of several hundred thousand very successful and privately happy people who have demonstrated this in recent decades and will continue to do so in the coming decades. You are not alone on this journey and your task is to implement day by day what you have planned and set out to do with the flow chart, as well as to control your world of thoughts, in addition to the discipline in the implementation plan.

This also includes being proud of yourself, appreciating yourself, and granting yourself the recognition, appreciation, and dignity that everyone deserves in the sense of self-care. You also have to look at this from the perspective of potential: **You have enormous potential.** And just as nothing is older than yesterday's success, I always say: Nothing is older than yesterday's failure. Just because you may have had some failures, you can't buy anything for it in the present and future. Just as you can't buy anything for past success. It's like in sports: The last season is the last season, a new chapter begins and you can actively shape, rewrite the story.

> **Tip**
>
> **The future is not yet written and in combination with your potential, your determination, and your diligence, you have all possibilities. In the age of digital transformation, nothing has changed about the fact that diligence, determination, reliability, resilience, and punctuality are still the virtues with which you can work towards success. Nothing has changed about this in the digital age either.**

As you can read, discipline is also the question of whether you are capable of mentally programming yourself and maintaining a permanently positive performance-ready mode. This can best be supported by simply making decisions that practically put you in a **discipline corset**.

Example: If I have the problem that I can't get anything done on the weekend, then I have to make the decision now that there is no five-day week, but that from now on there is a **seven-day week**. Your work week consists of seven days. It doesn't matter what day it is, you are productive every day. It may be that you develop a different productivity strategy on Saturday than on Thursday, where you may be employed in a company or in your own business. If you are self-employed, you are always self and constantly, there is always round-the-clock readiness required. Then you may not be on the road with customers, but then you are in thought. Conceptual thinking or strategic considerations are then part of the working time. But first of all, you should make it clear whether you can make the decision to establish the seven-day week for yourself for the next few years.

With this, you have a discipline corset. That means, the question doesn't even arise: Do I have an unproductive weekend ahead of me? Instead, you know, you have to push hard every day. Because conversely, if you know that you do nothing on a day, unless it is a day when you reward yourself for a previous performance, a work package or similar, then you will inevitably feel an unpleasant feeling. And this emotional trick forces you to do something after all. Welcome to the seven-day week. Try it out! At worst, you are the type for the 6-day week.

In the literature, there are different views on the topic of discipline. Baumeister and Tierney (2012) describe the power of discipline and the training possibilities of our will, while other authors (Brumlik 2007) discuss the dangers of abuse and exaggerated expectations of educational psychological effects. Problems with discipline in school (Rüedi 2002; Hoffmann 2009), in classroom management and violence prevention up to discipline in the former GDR (Krüger and Marotzki 1994) show the full breadth of the field of discipline. This book is about discipline as a basis for private and professional success, lasting and sustainable. And from this perspective, we look at the importance of working through your work packages in a disciplined manner every day in order to achieve the goals you have set for yourself.

Burghardt (2015) demonstrates that discipline and serenity are not opposites in order to be successful. Covey (2018) attributes the increase in effectiveness to discipline and planning, while Gross and Jungbauer-Gans (2007) show the factor of discipline as a building block of success in scientific careers. Lasko et al. (2005) see total self-responsibility in the individual for discipline, Hruschka et al. (2009) reinforce this by assessing that only iron discipline leads to long-term success, and Loch (1997) deals with "discipline or flexibility" in the interpretation of the implementation of discipline in the field of innovation, growth, and economy. They thus see that only a disciplined time, planning, and implementation strategy leads to success in private and professional goals. Flexibility and situational adjustments always exist, but this does not absolve one from staying on the ball daily and taking responsibility oneself.

Change of Perspective

1. Set high goals

There is always the possibility of failure, but much more dramatic is to look back years later and ask yourself: What if? My personal experience is that regardless of the project goal, you learn a lot along the way and even after the project, regardless of the result, you have expanded your network and can go into the next project with new energy. So you neither lose time nor energy, even if, in the worst case, you have failed. Rather, you have a learning curve, a learning efficiency, an expanded network, and can build the next attacks on this new foundation.

2. Willingness to give everything

When I was writing my first doctoral thesis in the Department of Oral and Maxillofacial Surgery while working and during the founding of my dental practice in Leverkusen, I worked the first years on Monday and Wednesday from 08:00 to 20:00. I was so tired in the evening that I hardly managed to continue writing the doctoral thesis. Then I decided to stay in the practice right after work and write on the doctoral thesis for another two hours, showered in the practice, and slept on the couch. And I did this twice a week for 3 years on Mondays and Wednesdays and was able to slightly increase my productivity in writing the doctoral thesis.

At that time, I was also attending further training and education on weekends, where sometimes there was not enough time to continue writing the doctoral thesis. After the doctoral thesis, I got used to staying in the practice at least twice a week for another 5 years, and then got up at seven in the morning, showered in the practice shower. I had new clothes with me and then also saved the time to drive home and drive back in the morning. So that was my way of reacting to this problem during this multi-year phase. And this discipline, doing everything to get closer to the goal, requires discipline, and this is reflected in decisions that are then unpleasant in a certain way.

You don't sleep so well on the couch. You are often a bit nervous at night in such a large health house, where I have the practice, because you feel a bit lost in such a large complex and sleep a bit alert, whether someone is sneaking around the practice at night or not. But in the end, after this goal was achieved, you look back and laugh inwardly at what an exciting and challenging time it was, the very personal journey. Time always flies by too quickly in retrospect, and it is precisely these personal sacrifices or the commitment that you have made that sweeten the memory a bit. You really gave everything and then it is all the more beautiful when you have achieved the goal.

3. The power of thoughts

I once met a company founder in Silicon Valley (USA) in 2015 who told me: "Yes, what this environment in Stanford and in the San Francisco Bay Area creates is that such a positive life mood arises that people not only work around the clock on their projects, but are so euphoric about the projects they are working on that they even dream about them at night, so that you practically generate "110 percent" time intensity when you work on the projects during waking hours and even dream about them at night."

This may sound a bit exaggerated and not everyone is a company founder, but the goal is to discipline your thoughts, think positively, and not doubt that you will achieve your goals. You can be enthusiastic about yourself, your projects, and others. An excellent basis for a great mindset.

4. Limited Lifetime

Lifetime is limited and thus the time to realize your dreams and visions is also limited. Do you really want to let external conditions and what others think prevent you from reaching your goal? That can't be serious.

Establish mental toughness towards yourself. This has nothing to do with people who are buzzing around you or with any external influences. This is an I-to-I story here. You have to be tough on yourself. Try to avoid anything that has a negative impact on your positive basic constitution. This can be depressive music, it can be bad news, it can be that you are currently surrounded by people who mentally drag you down, who see everything in a gloomy way and who actually only whine and complain all day and see everything as difficult, or people who don't trust you to do something.

You have to challenge yourself to ruthlessly implement the implementation plan derived from the time flow diagram. You have to commit to the seven-day week and the will to become a radical learning and working machine. No one but you can do it for you! Who can stop you then?

It's a competitive situation and if you fail today, it doesn't say anything about what tomorrow will be. Over the past 15 years, I have been fortunate to often travel to the USA, Asia, South Africa, and Europe and visit private and academic innovation environments. There I met

5 The Decision for the Personal Innovation Process

many people of different ages, 20-, 30-, 40-, 50-, 60-, 70-, 80-year-olds, who in their own way with their experiences of self-realization of their dreams and visions, their goals, be it company foundations, academic careers, scientific projects have implemented. And failure was always on the list, and the life paths have been very different. Some had to change the country, some had to change the industry, some had several projects that did not go well. And yet all have found success in their own way because they have disciplined their thoughts positively controlled, always believed in themselves and ultimately also delivered their daily work package to step by step approach the goal they have set and then achieve it.

Project termination is sometimes also an issue. In business, it is said that sometimes a project termination is more cost-effective than ruthlessly pulling through a project. But you should not have this project termination theory or this Plan-B theory on your radar at all, but you should manage your time well, you should then be tough on yourself in the implementation phase and implement what you have planned for the day and the week as a work package from the planning and also radically commit to having a goal and being willing to give everything for it. I can tell you from my own experience: I am now 50 and have achieved various academic goals, successfully completed various entrepreneurial activities for me and now have the next goals on the radar for the next few years, and this strategy, good planning, good presentation in writing and then really consistently delivering the work package day by day. And if there is a day that was not good, or a week where maybe you are sick or it doesn't work or for whatever reasons, then distribute the work packages to be made up to the following weeks and always see that you stay focused until the end, until the last day and achieve the goal.

Once you've pulled it off, you have a lot of self-confidence and can approach the next goals even more relaxed and confident. It's like an avalanche, you work your way through goal by goal and before you know it, ten, 20 years have passed and you think: Wow, I've managed all that, amazing. Yesterday I was still a student and today I am already a company founder, senior employee in a company or I am socially engaged.

Regardless of what the goals are, the goals are as colorful as life itself, as nature around us. You have the power and the potential, but you have to control your world of thoughts in a disciplined way and always keep yourself in a state of activity and confidence through positive thoughts and positive self-reflection, then it works. The essence is ultimately that life is much too short compared to what we all want to do and achieve. And it's nice, it keeps you in suspense to always set new goals and work on them. It's an exciting journey, an adventure. You get to know yourself better, you change and over the years the personal potential is revealed. Because the benchmark is not what others think or what others say to you about the successes, but:

- **How much of personal potential could one implement and materialize?**

That is actually the much more exciting question, to find out what is inside oneself and what achievements and activities one can develop over the years, of course with a positive influence on society and for customers or patients. But ultimately the foundation is a disciplined mental strength, where you are tough on yourself and implement what you have planned.

Figure 5.1 is intended to motivate you to keep track of what percentage of tasks you have completed and how

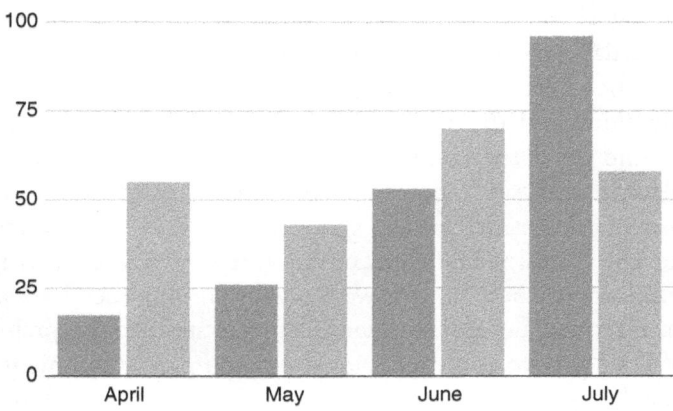

Fig. 5.1 "Documentation is key" according to Plugmann (own illustration)
This figure is meant to remind you to keep track of your performance, so you always have an overview.

satisfied you are with your own performance. This way, you maintain an overview.

5.3 The Next Goal: Nothing is Older than Yesterday's Success!

Now you have reached the goal, congratulations. Your commitment, the relentless effort day and night, on weekends and in most of your free minutes, the efforts, exhaustion and regeneration phases were the foundation and you can now rightly be proud of it. Enjoy this moment behind the finish line, the success, and make yourself aware of what you have achieved. Now is a good time for a reward!

To maintain the tension, it is necessary to keep the guiding star, the big overarching goal, in mind and use it as a magnet. Nothing is older than yesterday's success, the next goal awaits. If you now stagnate and rest lavishly on yesterday's successes, the decline begins. The competition does not sleep, the markets are globally under fire around the clock and the next start-up or the direct competitor around the corner are just waiting for you to enter a complacent, arrogant phase of self-overestimation and thus become negligent and less goal-oriented. A danger source for the performance slump after reaching a goal, which you have reached on your way to your guiding star (goal as an intermediate goal or stage), is to succumb to the praise of your private and professional environment. Comments like "How do you do that?", "Great, you're top" or "Does your day have 48 hours?" should be taken positively and gladly pass on the knowledge about your personal work and learning method, but please never take off. As soon as you leave the tension and competition mode level, you will no longer be focused, goal-oriented and aggressive.

You should also take the moment to report your perspective to people who congratulate you on this sensational success and want to give the impression that you and the success are due to luck or chance. This has the effect of self-motivation and reflection on your performance and endurance and increases self-confidence again.

> **Tip**
>
> **Report that you have been working towards this goal for many years and that this currently achieved goal is to be considered as an intermediate goal. It's like a train journey, just one station of many that are still to come and you are on your way to unfolding your actual potential. Explain that while others have enjoyed holidays, parties or a stress-free life in the past years, you have been pushing full throttle week after week, month after month and year after year under maximum effort, accepting deprivations and renunciations and regularly enduring states close to exhaustion. And all this without a guarantee of success**

> or any other security. You have worked hard for your goal by deciding years ago to become a permanent learning and working machine, to be productive 7 days a week, to maintain your network and to separate from "toxic people". You have continuously worked on your discipline, self-motivation and will. You have occasionally failed or not made progress and have never given up. You know today that you have only tapped a fraction of your personal potential.

5.4 Now Everything Depends on you—Give it Your All!

We have reached the end of this guide. I hope there were some impulses for you that provide you with the energy to enable a rocket start to your fixed star.

Finally, a few lines for your journey into the future: As children we have dreams, as teenagers ideas and during our education or studies these "dreams & ideas" come back in all variations. Then we are 25 or 30 years old and programmed in a certain way through our experiences and encounters with people. You have the right to emotionally delete, suppress and ignore this section from your brain. What counts exclusively is your decision in the present, how you reinvent yourself, change your behavior and start to become a permanent learning and working machine. You find the term "machine" unromantic?

Remember, it's a mindset. Of course, you are not a machine or a robot, and life consists of numerous facets, stages of life and personal design preferences. It is a mindset, a thought model, a level of communication with yourself, to set high goals and to achieve these self-set goals through radical implementation of the necessary goal and planning prerequisites.

Don't let naysayers, whiners, grumblers, enviers, people who radiate negative energy, and your own destructive thoughts stop you—never give up!

Figure 5.2 finally asks you to transform your mindset. Look at the FIXED STAR, what or who do you see? Remember, at the core it's about you:

The path to the goal is for most people, including myself, a long, hard, rocky and challenging path. There is no guarantee for a long life, happiness, fun or success. And no one really cares about your life and the goals you want

Fig. 5.2 "FIXED STAR—Transformation of the Mindset" according to Plugmann (own illustration). This figure shows you your FIXED STAR. Transform your mindset!

If you look at the FIXED STAR long enough, what or who do you see?

to achieve. You are on your own, even if you have a network. The shining moments take place alone and without social media, when you sit alone at your desk at 2 in the morning and study, get up at 5:30 in the morning or make the decision to forego vacation for 2 years in order to use the freed up financial resources for part-time studies. You can read this guide, exchange experiences with your network and philosophize with friends and family, but **you have to walk the last meter alone—your life, your decision! Now everything depends on you—give it your all!! Good luck!!!**

In 2022 we will organize webinars and seminars on this complex of topics, we will see each other. Stay tough, you are in competition with yourself, time for action, full throttle mentality, radical time, planning and implementation management, separation from "toxic people", become a permanent learning and working machine in 7-day mode, never give up and off you go.

References

Baumeister, R. F., & Tierney, J. (2012). *Die Macht der Disziplin: Wie wir unseren Willen trainieren können*. Campus.

Brumlik, M. (2007). *Durch Unterwerfung zur Freiheit. Bernhard Buebs reaktionäre Vergangenheitsbewältigung.* (pp. 52–75). Vom Missbrauch der Disziplin. Antworten der Wissenschaft auf Bernhard Bueb.

Burghardt, B. (2015). Disziplin. In *Gelassenheit gewinnen-30 Bilder für ein starkes Selbst* (pp. 65–68). Springer Gabler.

Covey, S. R. (2018). *Die 7 Wege zur Effektivität: Prinzipien für persönlichen und beruflichen Erfolg*. GABAL Verlag GmbH.

Gross, C., & Jungbauer-Gans, M. (2007). Erfolg durch Leistung? Ein Forschungsüberblick zum Thema Wissenschaftskarrieren. *Soziale Welt, 58*(4), 453–471.

Hoffmann, C. (2009). *Disziplinschwierigkeiten in der Schule* (pp. 21–107). VS Verlag.

Hruschka, P., Rupp, C., & Starke, G. (2009). Agilität und Disziplin. In: *Agility kompakt. IT kompakt.* Spektrum Akademischer Verlag. https://doi.org/10.1007/978-3-8274-2204-0_5.

Krüger, H. H., & Marotzki, W. (1994). Pädagogik und Erziehungsalltag in der DDR – Eine Einführung. In *Pädagogik und Erziehungsalltag in der DDR* (pp. 7–15). VS Verlag.

Lasko, W. W., Busemann, F., & Busch, P. (2005). Disziplin: Selbstverantwortung. In *Zehnkampf-Power für Manager* (pp. 53–66). Gabler.

Loch, C. (1997). Disziplin oder Flexibilität? In *Management von Innovation und Wachstum* (pp. 184–201). Gabler.

Rüedi, J. (2002). Disziplin in der Schule. In *Plädoyer für ein antinomisches Verständnis von Disziplin und Klassenführung.* Haupt.

GPSR Compliance
The European Union's (EU) General Product Safety Regulation (GPSR) is a set of rules that requires consumer products to be safe and our obligations to ensure this.

If you have any concerns about our products, you can contact us on

ProductSafety@springernature.com

In case Publisher is established outside the EU, the EU authorized representative is:

Springer Nature Customer Service Center GmbH
Europaplatz 3
69115 Heidelberg, Germany

www.ingramcontent.com/pod-product-compliance
Lightning Source LLC
LaVergne TN
LVHW040741250326
834688LV00031B/381